VOICES FROM

ANCIENT BETHLEHEM

JODERE
GROUP
SAN DIEGO, CALIFORNIA

VOICES FROM ANCIENT BETHLEHEM

A DIALOGUE WITH JESUS AND THE TWELVE APOSTLES

Copyright © 2003 by JODERE GROUP, INC.

CIP data available from the Library of Congress

ISBN 1-58872-094-2

06 05 04 03   4 3 2 1
First printing, December 2003

PUBLISHED BY:

JODERE GROUP, INC.
P.O. Box 910147
San Diego, CA 92191-0147
(800) 569-1002
www.jodere.com

PRINTED IN THE UNITED STATES OF AMERICA

CONTENTS

CHAPTER TWO:
THE GOSPEL OF THE TWELVE DISCIPLES 53

THE GOSPEL ACCORDING TO PETER................... 54

VOICES FROM
ANCIENT BETHLEHEM

INTRODUCTION

❧

S oul travel is that great art that has long been taught and practiced by mystics and seers with unerring vision through the ages to discern the truth of God's will and ways. It is the practice of moving the consciousness out of the body to talk, communicate, and study with teachers and masters of other times and places that now dwell and serve within the inner realms. The student of this technique does learn, through patient study and application, to place the attention beyond the physical consciousness and in a higher place where truth and love may be directly perceived and understood. Thus have all great masters and teachers proficient in this skill brought back great Truth to their followers to guide them firmly and truly on the path back to God.

I am a student of this ancient art and science and as part of my regular spiritual practice do engage in quiet contemplation and seek the wisdom and guidance of the masters and teachers of the inner realms. It was in this manner that I was approached and it was asked if I would do a great service to the Christ to bring to light an updated version of His great truth and teachings and that of His trusted Disciples. The Christ did feel that the time had come that His followers and the world were in need of new inspiration and life to inspire and energize the great tradition that had been built in His name. Times had changed, and His words of Truth needed to be updated to reflect these new conditions.

Though Christianity is not my path, I, of course, did consent to humbly serve Him in His request, and with the utmost gratitude and respect do I offer these, His words, to all readers, that they might find solace and hope in their truth and light. I only serve as scribe and recorder of all that He does wish to say, and not as the source or interpreter. Jesus offers these, His words, to the world as His gift in troubled times, and hopes that all will find comfort and inspiration to continue on the great path home to heaven, where He joyously does await them.

With gratitude and appreciation,

THE SCRIBE

NOTE: Jesus was asked that His flock may doubt the authenticity of these words, and He understood how charlatans tend to bend the spiritual substance of His name and works. Jesus' reply to the latter statement was:

The mind is always looking for an argument,
The heart is always looking for peace.
No man or woman can serve both in life.
One or the other will guide
Each seeker to different ends.
Those who know me will know these words belong to me,
The Christ.

CHAPTER ONE

JESUS' SCRIPTURES

OPENING THE DIALOGUE

Scribe, this book must come from the heart of you. It is only you that has the ears and eyes to truly see what did transpire. Many have been the trips I have made to stand before the Lords of Time to answer for others' deeds, and now is the time to set all straight and relieve me of my burden. When this book is given to the hearts of man, then shall there be no reason for me to ever again be called to task for the deeds of others. It shall be their ignorance only that blots the light and brings them to their knees.

You honor me with your willingness to assume my task, yet none of my Brotherhood still have the eyes or ears to find the hidden truth. You must travel deep within the ages and bring back the great truths of old. Then shall you know what truly happened and be able to share it with the world.

WHY THE FATHER
BROUGHT ME TO EARTH

I was sent to bring back balance into the hearts of man. All had descended into darkness, and no hearts bore true warmth for their neighbor. The path of certain destruction was before all that roamed the earth, and I was sent to mend the great rift that had separated man from his true self. I was taught the frequencies and motions that would open the hearts of man that he might hear again the voice of his true nature. Great were the mysteries I did learn, yet all were more interested in the healings and lifting of curses.

This was the time before the pharaohs had descended to build the great pyramids in the sand when Gods still walked the earth with their shoulders even to man. The time slipped by and the lords of my line realized the error that had occurred as planned. Man had made many poor choices and the decision was made to let all continue in its course to see if the ship would be righted. But man had lost his eyes and ears and thus was unable to find again his one true path.

I was to be sent as a messenger to bring back the secrets to finding those senses, which would return man to the true path. I would bring the heart of love and open it to its oneness. Then would all rejoice and return again to the path. Yet it was not to be. Man had passed too far into the darkness of illusion, and my best was not sufficient. I left the earth with my mission unfulfilled and men with eyes for power did bend my words unto their own devices. The words that now exist under the banner of my name do not reflect or resemble the heart of that which gave them. You must let all man know the true words that I did speak and of what remained unspoken.

The love I gave to my own flock was lost when the teachings faded. All that I did to open their hearts was for naught as my words were lost and bent. Those with hearts that sought of power did use my name in vain, and the bubbling springs I had unleashed were quickly dried and closed. Thus is it that you have come to open again their gentle trickles. That once you leave and others follow, a roaring torrent should ensue.

OF THE BIBLE AND OTHER TEXTS

The Bible and other texts have become tenet books of the church, and many have found great truth and wisdom there. However, the greatest truth of all is not to be found in those pages, which are not the true words of my heart, but in these my true Scriptures that I do give with love for my flock as they are recorded by the Scribe. However, it is to the discerning eye and heart of the good student to determine what is to be held and believed and what is to be discarded. The words contained within this book and written by the Scribe are my truth and that of my Disciples, as we have told it to him in each and every word. The truth of our hearts may be felt and known by the energy of the words upon the page. And those who take the prayers and passages into their hearts in quiet contemplation will know that what is said is real.

This great book of the Scribe is to be used together with the Bible and other works of merit by other authors to guide the student on the path in their own journey of discovery and understanding. Truth and knowledge are won by the brave heart and valorous soul, not given to the meek who huddle in the corner awaiting the light of God. So, the able student shall use this text as the starting place and from there go and read all others and compare and contemplate and seek within his or her own heart of what is the truth of the ways of God. For it is by discipline and trial and error that wisdom and understanding are wrought from the fire of confusion and ignorance, and thus shall the student rapidly grow and progress truly and mightily upon the path.

OF ANGELS, CHERUBS, AND SERAPHIMS

Of angels and cherubs and others, there can be no doubt of their true existence and function, for without the protection of benevolent forces, man should truly find himself in a living horror of ways and evil devices. The angel of each and every person is selected for its mission based on its skills and past associations and is charged with helping each soul to progress forward on the path through those experiences that help to temper it as Soul and lead it back to heaven.

However, though each angel is assigned to one or several or a group of persons, it can only do so much. Man is on earth and in the physical body to learn to master the right to exercise his free will, and an angel or guardian can under no circumstances abrogate that sacred right. Thus, most do not have the ears to hear or eyes to see of the subtle voices and myriad signs that angels do leave as hints as to the right and proper course. Some do come in dreams, but these are properly understood but by few and are usually misinterpreted. Some do come as gentle nudges or intuitive urges, and some do come as wakeful coincidences and occurrences that point truly to the proper way.

As the student does grow in wisdom and awareness, he does learn through trial and error the proper way to interpret his angel's symbols and make his way within the world to avoid disaster and misfortune. The angel of your soul is always near and does always hear your words, though you usually are not aware of it and seldom hear its answer.

When you do beseech of its aid in the name of the Father, it does take your true request and so put it within the very Spirit of God, for resolution in HIS ways, in the manner that HE considers most beneficial for the spiritual development of the soul in question. HE rarely does answer superficial pleas for fame and glory, for rarely is this an experience needed for the further unfoldment of man. Often as well will HE not interfere in circumstances of the man's own making, for when man does bring painful circumstances upon himself, from this or some past life, it is not the function of an angel to remove those lessons from man, for how then would he truly progress upon the path and what would be his purpose here but to learn those painful lessons.

The angel, rather, is about to ensure that man's lessons do not exceed his capacity to succeed in them, and to see that the details of events and circumstances that must transpire in his life between himself and certain others do indeed take place. The angel also often does work to make sure that the passing away of the body does transpire at the certain time and place that is designated, and so the soul does pass gently to the other side.

The true presence and merit of the protector may only be observed by careful and discerning eyes, for its language and deeds are subtle and often do elude the observation of even the cleverest minds. Truly, the best way to see the workings of your angel for you is with a calm and peaceful countenance to observe all events about you, and as they do unfold to be sensitive to specific occurrences that do have a little energetic charge or funny manner of how they do transpire, like a memory faded and then remembered, or a remarkable coincidence that feels somehow different. Then to truly take the keys and gifts as they are presented and to follow them onward and see where they do truly lead. And thus shall ultimate success with challenges and difficult situations teach you to trust in the recognition and teachings of your heart. Thus do the angels function and truly look over man.

THE NATURE OF LOVE

Of now I speak of love, for this is the heart of all the matters. My Scriptures do begin, and we address the most important question first.

What is the nature of love? It is that thing we do constantly ponder as to the true nature of our wonders. What is it that makes us feel and gaze longingly at others?

There is a code within the heart that has to it many layers. Within each mask that is peeled off comes closer to the great truth. I have seen 1,000 years and more and do know a few of the answers, and of love I can tell you this: Each heart is locked, as if with a code, that determines all its answers. All that is seen and known in life is regulated by this center. The frequencies that are sent and received do create the world around us. One who is open and bearing forth with truth and love will find himself with his brothers. One who is closed and hard of heart will live fearfully among the tigers.

Of the love between the sexes, little is understood. They seek a brief glimpse of the Lord within each other's clutches and embraces. Man and his twin must truly learn that there is a good and healthy order. First must he share his heart with God before he can truly share it with another. Not until there is no fear can he see to what his nature is to give of complete and total love and support without any fear of repercussion. When both have found a higher cause, then shall they find each other and slumber peacefully in each other's arms safe from all the world.

Though it is hard, this is the way to finding the true happiness with another. There must be no fear, but only love, for one without the other. When there is fear, then one does cling and greatly offend the other. This creates an imbalance of love, and one must sway away to make all equal. When each is strong in his own heart, then is there complete balance. If one should lose the higher self, then the lower laws do push him, and all the good and warmth of love is quickly rent asunder.

For children, there is a different sort of love within the heart. It is the rule and law of reproduction that the children must learn at the hand of their fathers and mothers. This is a love of a different tone, yet it is not stronger or weaker. The child must know that the love is born so deep it cannot falter, and truly still must the parent know that the firm and loving hand of guidance to set the child well upon the proper path cannot falter.

The young children must rely on the firm hand of the parent's love to guide them along their early paces. The mind is young, and the modern world is fraught with meddlesome places. Though a young boy or girl may not always like the father's faces, he or she must respect the wisdom there and yet remain always in proper places. When the boy is grown and has become a man, then might he direct himself to his own places. Upon this day, a bond has changed and the father and son do move to different places. A freedom now has come of age to direct their own affairs. The boy may leave and move swiftly on to begin with his own experiences.

Of love between the siblings, I can say this: The brothers come into this world to continue on with cycles. They are within each other's grasp to resolve all past life issues. To look upon your kin with love, and never with crossness, does truly bring all to a close and speed all to the heart of all matters. It is natural for there to be difficult times amongst them, yet when they are grown up and well, they must understand the cycles that bind them. Siblings are to seek within the true cause of their arrangements. In this way shall they end the cycles and continue ever onward. The key to understanding all is to pursue the light of the heart. As with this, and in all else, this is all that matters.

Teach the children that they should know that there is but one sacred lesson: to love and serve the One above and always give to each other. This lesson is a difficult one but must be learned beyond reason. The many things that we do see to fight are not but all illusions. When they do finally know the way and truly see the reasons, then shall all the veils lift, and they shall know the seasons.

Of man and strangers, I can say these simple rules. Treat each as if he were your own, and shelter him in all seasons. The gift of love does never end and always does return to you. The hearts of man do fear the night and what the stranger brings them, but their great fear is all there is, for love is what yet binds them. Walk not with the tigers, but with your brothers that all might take your hand and carry on as if were all a part of greater circles.

As to man and God, there is this: Man yearns to know how he should pray to know of his great savior. I tell you this—that all is naught for what is it within us. There is already in our hearts the key to secret treasures. All that we think and others say must not truly bind us. God is you, and you are HIM, and that is all there is to it. The only thing that stands between is the fear that keeps you from it.

Devote a portion of each day to quietly seeking of HIM. There are many ways that you can proceed and each of them is valid. There is no single path to God except love. Many lands and many faces do carry many messages. Saviors come and speak of what is true to their own races.

Let me be clear on this: Love is the one great true path that brings all peoples and races together and guides them home again to God. There is not a single source of all truth and love, for many have brought its message in different forms, at different times, in the history of man. It was my mission to come in my time and bring of the truth of love that I did know to give it to those who did need it. But others, too, have come to serve of those who did need of the truth as well, yet in a form and person that the people could allow to enter into their hearts.

And so, though there are those within the church who do say mine way is the only path to God, this is not true. For there is but one God, with many paths to HIS door, and mine is but one of them. Any path of merit that does teach love as its central premise and theme is one that can guide the seeker closer to God's heart, and any who do claim theirs is the only way do speak from a heart of fear and desire only to maintain of their control and power. For love seeks to give of life and compassion and understanding and is tolerant of all paths and ways that are its brothers. All who do seek of truth and the infinite glory of God with love in their hearts shall be successful in their endeavors— whatever is the name of the path or savior that they do choose.

Many have been the great disgraces of ignorance and injustice. The inquisition and the stake were two of the worst and gravest. The Spanish Inquisition was a travesty of justice and investigation that the church did wrongly use to rid itself of its enemies and ensure of the propagation of its dogma and doctrine. The church has long held a great fear of new and true ideas, lest it threaten the power and control that so many have worked so hard to achieve. The stake, too, was an example of the cruelty and inhumane treatment of those the church did despise—that by intimidation and great shows of power and force, it should keep its enemies at bay.

This is not the way of love, compassion, or understanding, which were truly the mark of the heart of my teachings. Power and control do never serve to liberate the hearts of men and any who do employ them do only further the bondage and illusion created by the forces of darkness. In my name have many burned and much has been my burden. If ever any should again do injustice in my name, they shall never enter heaven. Though this seems rash, it must be so, for power has corrupted. All that I strived to build and grow now has been perverted. You must strive to know the love of God else all is lost to you. There is no other way to HIM except through your heart. Listen to my words and seek a way that you might truly know them.

OF GOD, LOVE, AND OTHER LIFE-FORMS

This I do say about God: As to other life that comes upon us, I can say this. Long has the Angelic Order of the Grey Robes of old protected earth and maintained balance. There is intelligent life in other places, and soon does it come to us. Do not greet others in fear. Show them of your heart and work diligently to find good solutions.

Fear further divides us from the heart of what is ours. When they do come from outer space, you must prepare to greet them. They will have superior arms, and you will not be able to defeat them. Greet the saviors, and give them your heart that they should lead you to safety. This shall be the key to know that the planet will find safety.

MY COMING

I did truly receive the baptism of my initiation at the watery hands of John the Baptist who did induct me under that ancient and sacred rite. Though its true ways and power are lost today, in that time and place, it was a key to greater wisdom, love, and power. When he did perform the rite and hold me under water, there did come to me a vision of great and wondrous light, and I did see all the universes of God open to my understanding. Then did I know what I must do and set upon my journeys.

For 40 days and 40 nights, I wandered in the desert to regain my balance and composure else all would have thought me truly mad. Then guided by divine providence and mine own intuition did I begin to seek in earnest all the wisdom that I did know that I would need. After seven years of wandering and searching, I was finally ready to begin my great work and did return to Jerusalem to commence with my mission.

I Will Teach Thee to Pray

A daily prayer that may be used by all does have of many benefits. It does, at the early dawn, serve to create around the student an aura of love and protection that does follow him throughout the day and keep him from harm and out of reach of those with bad intentions. Thus do I give this prayer to you for your well-being and your protection that you should repeat it each day upon rising and during moments of quiet reflection to keep my love and protection about you always.

For the new prayer it shall be this:

Prayer of Hope for the Living

There comes upon the breast of Man, a great hope and an awakening.
This hope shall be the name of Christ, to end of all the suffering.

I shall guide those home again, that truly seek the healing,
For their hearts are rent and broken down with all the years of stealing.

When there does come within the heart a question of the matter,
You must but only call my name, and I shall always be there.

You are not forgotten nor left alone, to stand and face the dangers,
I am with love about the world, and always shall I be there.

These shall be my words for all to repeat and say. Though it sounds unconventional, it must be a great departure from my previous words, which were not of my own heart.

THE QUESTION OF MORALITY

Of the knowledge of right and wrong, I can say this: Within the heart, there lies the great wisdom to discern even the most difficult of questions. All that you must do is quietly go within and gently repeat my name. After the time when all is calm and you have found forgiveness, then see my face and gently place the question before my visage. Your heart shall truly tell you of the proper answer. With time and practice, you will find that the heart does become an able master. Then shall you walk with friends and escape the claws of tigers.

There are many different things to consider upon all questions, yet the mind does not provide all answers. There is a higher intelligence that speaks through the heart and often defies rational logic. The true knowledge of the ways of the universe is a mixture of science and faith. Together, they hold all the answers for each exists within the other, and neither may stand without. There shall come a day when all this shall be clearly understood.

OF THE SOUL AND NEW LIFE

The pregnancy in a woman has long been a sacred act of man and love to bring another soul into being to share and participate in God's great plan. But there are a myriad of factors to be considered in the decision of what actions to take once a fetus has been conceived.

During the term of pregnancy, the soul does enter and leave the fetus at will as it does test and become accustomed to its new vessel and home. It is a game of play for the soul to come in and experience of the wonders of a physical body and then leave again to celestial realms to make final preparations and say goodbye to friends. However, the soul does not permanently enter the body until the body does have the strength and will to independently live of its own breath and means. It is not fully anchored inside the vessel until the vessel is capable of supporting it of its own accord. Thus must any decision with regard to the soul of a new or unborn vessel be considered in this way.

The issue is one for the mother, as it is a matter kept within her heart and born within her body and temple, and none do have the right or power to dictate the actions or proper course of another as it does relate to the sanctity of her own body. Though this is a controversial matter, each soul has had during its many lifetimes the right and responsibility for the conception and birth of new life, and each must learn of its own decisions how to pass through this process. And so man does never have the right of domain over the body of woman, and so must she be left to make her own decision with the knowledge I have given here.

THE COURAGE TO FIND GOD

It is a common misconception that the timid and meek do find the greatest favor in heaven, yet this is not the case. God is found and won by the brave and valorous of heart who do always seek of HIS radiance and glory without any fear in their hearts. This is not a statement or judgment of physical strength or prowess—but of the heart of courage that does drive the devoted student to stride proudly and strongly into the face of all fears—and to conquer all that stands in his way and prevents him from finding God.

God and HIS love and wisdom come to those who will let no fear or any other factor stand between him and the Father. God does not seek and give HIMSELF willingly to those who sit idly by and wait. HE is won on the field of battle against the demons of darkness who do seek to keep man from HIS arms. The mighty illusions are those things that do cause us fear and delay us on our path, and the fearless lover of God shall never be deterred from seizing of his goal and he shall be the one to return to the Father's side in heaven in a blaze of heavenly glory and find the heart and love of God opened within his breast to be seen and shared with all the world. Do not sit and wait for God to find you. Open your heart and face what does blind you to HIS love and all victory and success shall be yours.

THE DIVINE LAWS

The Divine Laws are these:

FIRST: That no man should violate the free will or right to choice of another.

SECOND: That all men should at all times respect the right of others to worship in the manner they do see fit.

THIRD: That none shall deprive another of the right to life and happiness.

FOURTH: That all should respect the right of each to continue on their own path, and in their own way, and at their own pace back to heaven.

FIFTH: That each man should always do what he does solemnly vow.

SIXTH: That none shall put asunder the truth or light that God does bring to this earth through his Sons and Saviors.

These are the Divine Laws that must be learned and abided by.

The Great Illusions

The great illusions that do plague the peace and progress of man are truly these:

> 1) **GREED**: That unnatural desire to possess merely for the sake of owning in amount and for true reason that does exceed what is required for basic comfort and function.

> 2) **LUST**: The unnatural desire in man to consume any of the pleasures for reasons of satisfaction alone and for the sheer joy of the experience without any higher purpose. This is an unnatural expression of a natural function that has been perverted to an unhealthy level.

> 3) **ATTACHMENT**: The fear that comes of being too concerned or connected to a thing or person, which does truly lead one to make poor and unhealthy decisions.

> 4) **VANITY**: That attachment to the importance of the self that does give rise in a man to the belief that he is in some way superior to his brother and does cause him to take public or visible action to demonstrate this belief.

> 5) **PRIDE**: That arrogance of opinion in one's own accomplishment and power that does lead one to proclaim and exhibit what he does truly believe to be his superiority over another, though this is a false belief.

6) **ANGER**: The deadliest of all illusions during my time, and the focus of my ministry, this was greatly seen and known as its twins of hatred and fear, and thus the fury and rage of this sixth great illusion did often rise in men's hearts like a beast that was out of control and sought only to destroy its wielder.

Thus were the six great illusions truly known.

THE FOCUS OF MY MINISTRY

My ministry was truly focused on anger and fear, though this is not so prevalent today, for time and circumstances have greatly changed over the past 2,000 years. Today, greed and vanity and pride do truly drive the illusions that separate us from truth. The media and images and voices do all tell us of what it is that should truly make us happy, yet all of this is false, for material things and riches shall never see to help a man truly find the love and shelter of God. These are mere contrivances to bind him more closely to the darkness that does surround him and keep without the light. Thus must all seekers today be most careful not to be deceived by false images but to keep all comforts and pleasures in balance and perspective and so remain on the middle path and truly devoted to God.

EXTRICATION FROM THE GREAT ILLUSIONS

For those who do find themselves obsessed and engaged in one illusion or another, I can say truly this: To, in your imagination, play the extremes of that circumstance or pleasure forward to its furthest point, and then to place yourself mentally in that state, and search your heart to know if true and unalterable happiness will truly be found there, for those who are honest in their hearts will see that no illusions, no matter how great or pleasurable or good, shall ever be able to quench truly the burning desire for the love of God which is lodged deep in each and every heart. Thus might those obsessed with pleasures and the vices truly find their way to freedom.

For those who care not of their indulgences and who do not heed these admonishments, I do say this: That the pursuit only of pleasure and lower forms of happiness without regard to the development and unfoldment of your immortal soul shall only create more lifetimes of unhappiness and pain to unravel the misdeeds of this day and to learn the lessons that are put off and avoided or ignored in the pursuit only of pleasure. Thus must each truly face and overcome all unpleasant situations, and seek happiness and comfort in equal and balanced measure with the pursuit of spiritual goals, for this truly is the one way to follow in the Christ's footsteps and to the Father return home.

THE BOATMAN COMETH

To those who find that they are owned,
By dark forces or dark angels.

I give to you this single poem,
To aid you in your anguish.

These forces do so render you,
Without the aid of angels.

And I do come to rescue you,
And take you home to greatness.

This shall be the poem of salvation to aid of those addicted to drugs or other vices.

OF THOSE SEEKING WORLD PEACE

Man exists on earth to garner the difficult and sometimes painful lessons of experience that temper soul to the fine and polished metal that truly, in its softly glowing luster, reflects the perfect glory of God. The trials and experiences that man does need to see and learn his lessons are rarely won or understood in the garden paradise of heavenly pleasures, for there is little incentive when all is well to seek of better ways and greater wisdom. And so does man find himself upon the earth and confronted by many challenges. This is the purpose and nature of the physical worlds—and of earth in particular. Its wars and conflicts and trials are the true and natural essence of its nature to fulfill the role and mission for which it was conceived.

Those who do struggle for world peace do have well-intentioned motives, but the goal of their success may ever remain elusive, for it is not within the mission or purpose or destiny of our planet. Earth shall continue onward in the natural cycle of its progression until the end of this great cycle of God, and then will all again be returned to the long night of God until HE does again awaken and begin a new great cycle of birth.

But for those who now do strive to create peace on earth, I say this: Your efforts would be better served to spend wisely of your time and efforts to teach all truly of the ways and laws of God, for as they gain in consciousness and awareness, then will all problems of tyranny and unfairness naturally disappear. To try and change the actions of others to conform to your vision of what is the proper way and means to act is a gross violation of Divine Law and only serves as a vehicle and expression of the ego.

The greatest good can be truly done by showing love and abiding by the laws of God in your own life, and by this way being an example to all of the true and proper way of acting. Those who are bent on saving the world and clamor for world peace and peace

between nations are sadly deluded by a low level of spiritual understanding and unfoldment, for truly are all the strife and troubles of
the world the very means by which God's children do learn their
lessons and awaken to a better path and a vision of the way to truly
return home.

HOW TO FIND
YOUR MISSION IN LIFE

Each soul that comes upon the earth is truly here to fulfill its role
in life. There are predetermined plans and roles that each has agreed
to fulfill. The Angelic Robes above have given each a great task that
shall lead them rapidly onward. For each, it is their great responsibility to understand what it is that must be done. It cannot be learned
by faith alone but must be undertaken.

When one wishes to learn of his mission, he must be patient and
look carefully about him. It may often take time to get to that place
where it can be realized with clarity. Each day, one must go quietly
within and seek the truth of the heart. Repeat my name and go
within and seek the heart of the matter. When all is quiet and you feel
the din within subsiding, then gently put your question upon your heart
and let my light envelop it. Once the words have been consumed by
the great light of love, then take that love back into your heart and
slowly try to feel it. With time and patience, this shall be the way to
have all revealed to you. If you seek me with love in your heart and
openness in your mind, I shall come to you. For this is the way to know
what you have agreed to do in coming home.

OF PROPER DECISIONS

Of the way to find your mission, I have already spoken. Of direction is a different matter, for this pertains to the ways of making right decisions in all daily matters. Do not think too long on all your choices. Truly the proper course is always to be found in the heart. Ask yourself this one question: Is this act being taken in the love of another's wishes or to put power and illusion between us? Will this decision to act be considered true and just upon honest reflection? These are not things that come naturally to man with such a mind as he has developed but must be surpassed and cultivated as the higher faculty that it truly is.

Love is a greater faculty in man than the mind, for soul truly dwells above the mental plane, and is a place of higher truth and glory, and all would be wise to learn of how the inner worlds are structured and of their function and purpose. Man must learn that the heart does give the purest course of action to most rapidly climb onward toward its true home. God awaits those with bold and pure hearts to find their way back to HIM.

Often, it may be difficult to know the proper direction. Man must learn to go within and hear the true voice of soul. It is a voice that speaks softly through the heart and may be heard in quiet contemplation. To find your own true voice, you must find time each day to quietly go within and put my name gently upon your heart. Repeat it softly to yourself until you fall into a steady rhythm. When a time has passed and when you shall truly know, then shall you stop and relax and listen for the true wisdom of your gentle heart and it shall command you onward. God does watch and await your return.

OF DOING NO HARM

Of "do not harm," I will say this: There is much complexity about the issue of blood drawn of others, but this must be understood clearly. No man has the right to encroach on the space of another. If a man should forcibly make haste against you, you must preserve your life and sanctity and defend yourself against an aggressor. There is no glory to God in onward conquering others. The Holy Wars were not an act of faith, but a move to conquer others. But this wins no glory in heaven.

As to all other matters, the intent is the key, and there shall be no deceiving the Angelic Principalities. You truly reap what you do sow, and your intention in defense of what you hold dear must be pure. There is no glory in being martyrs and allowing others to rob you of your life. In difficult times, one must take measures to ensure the safety of home, country, and family. By treaties and other acts of diplomacy may outward expansion occur, but force of arms does sow bad seeds and lead to utter desolation. Whole countries may reap the seeds of the leaders who govern their actions. Take great care whom you do allow to decide for you, and do not make the grave error of the Germans and allow the darkness to overrun your heart and blind you.

OF HEALING AND MIRACLES

Many were the cures I did perform upon my day, and would that I had been wiser. Much was the cause and effect I did create from interfering with the angels' plans. Many have I gone and prayed for mercy for my healings. The one who is healed must truly be aware and accept responsibility for the changes. The only exception to this rule is this: The payment made may be shifted with the consent of the Angelic

Robes above. They must be consulted, and the man must know fully to what he is agreeing. Then may an illness be lifted and swayed to alternate directions.

Illness in many is often a symptom of the endless unseen cycle of cause and effect, and thus a current condition within the body may be known to have its seed and roots in those of previous actions. A healer may be able to move the effect of the cause in question to a different area and means of payment that the energy due for the cause may still be repaid but in another manner. This may only be done with the consent of the person and that of those involved from the realms of inner heavens. Once payment for a cause has been shifted to another area and the illness has been cured and lifted, then if that person does break the covenant of their agreement, this illness should return and may not be shifted again but must run its natural course.

Another way to say this is thus: Man may be healed by God or Christ or another in a miraculous or unknown way, but the grace given in this instance does come with a price, for all balance of energy and cause and effect must always be preserved. Once the healing is done and the illness removed somewhere, that energy must be dissipated or balanced.

Sometimes, the Christ or healer may take the energy of the illness upon himself and hold it for later dispersal in a manner of his own choosing, or sometimes it may be burned by himself in his own daily affairs and means as an act of love to the one whom he has healed. If the Christ or healer does balance the energy himself, then it is gone and the one who is healed shall forever remain so. However, if the payment is merely shifted to another part of the person's life, and that person should break the covenant of the agreement for its movement, then the original affliction should return and no hope shall he ever have again.

My Prayer, Song, and Gethsemane

The event of my arrest was truly known and foretold, and had been given to me in a dream by the great Archangel Gabriel. Not the specific details—but of what would generally occur. It was not heavy on my mind until that fateful night when we were all gathered in the Garden, and there was a knock upon the door. Then did I know that all would soon rapidly occur. Thus did I return and quickly initiate the Disciples, for I now had no choice left but to put them on their own paths. All time of teaching was over, and they would truly be left to their own ways. Then I did bid them return upon the morrow to share our final Supper, which I did know was truly to be my last. Then I did kneel and pray to the Father to truly take me home. And this is what I did say:

> *Heavenly Father, I art THOU Son,*
> *And I do truly call YOU.*
> *My deeds and actions have been done,*
> *And I now am called to pay the price.*
>
> *Though I have truly failed YOU,*
> *I bid YOU hold me near.*
> *And not forget my love for YOU,*
> *When the end is cold and near.*
>
> *I am YOUR Son from heaven,*
> *And I have come to do YOUR work.*
> *I did not do all things,*
> *But have given the love I could.*
>
> *Now the Romans do send me,*
> *Back to YOUR home above.*
> *I pray do not here leave me,*
> *Without YOUR great true love.*

Thus did I beg of the Father not to abandon me in my final hour, and thus did HE speak and agree to remove me from the body as I was raised aloft. Thus did I quietly slip from my shell as the soldiers did begin their duties and so felt no pain or suffering as the end did slowly come. When the body was removed and placed within the cave, I did return briefly to finalize all things. Then upon leaving, I did take it with me that none might bear it forth to use it in unseen ways. This is what truly did transpire and occur.

OF THE LAST SUPPER

Of the Chalice of the Last Supper, I can say this: that I did truly create it out of wood and pewter to serve as my own Cup upon the long roads that I did know I would soon travel, but this was not to be the case. When we were all gathered there and I did have to tell all what was to come and soon transpire, there was a depth of despair so profound and deep that I did need a boon to give them all to lift their sagging spirits. Thus did I reach for my own Cup and fill it with my blood, and utter the sacred incantation to bind us all together in love and brotherly unity. Thus did we break bread and in our hearts did agree, and did commit to do our works together even unto the time that our missions and the cycles had completed, and all should be finally said and done, and we gathered together.

I did take the Cup and entrust it to Peter that he should find a final home for it to be kept safe and rest. It now is well-hidden and protected in England. There is a noble order there that has kept it hidden for lo these many years and dedicated to its service. Now, a new age is upon us and a new time does come for a great rebirth and awakening of man, and the Cup must be returned from whence it came. Long has it served its purpose, but now all things do change and the ship must be righted upon its course.

OF THE SACRED RELICS

Of the Chalice and the Grail, there is this: The Chalice was that sacred Cup that the Disciples did use to drink of my blood during the Last Supper. The Grail is a stone with writing upon the edge that is the earthly incarnation that represents the consciousness of that state sometimes known as the "Universal" or "Christ" or "Buddha consciousness." The stone was given to Peter upon his travels and later passed to Benjamin to begin the Grail Line. I did direct Peter in his dreams where it might be found, and it has remained hidden ever since. It has written upon it the names of all the knights ever to hold it in their hand, for to touch it truly does one have to be of pure heart and initiated into the Circle's ways else it shall lead to certain death. It does now reside with the Chalice in that town where both are hidden and well-guarded.

THE SHROUD OF TURIN

It is truly I upon the Shroud that does now lie hidden within the dark walls of the museum of the Brotherhood, for they do keep the sacred relic hidden from harm's great way. They have been its protector for many years, and have done their duties well, but now this relic, too, must be returned to its home in Israel. The church fathers do truly know that this is so. When my body was lying lifeless within the cave and it was truly covered by the Shroud, all did lie quietly and seemingly without life. But as I did descend again into the body, I did pass through the gentle Shroud and the act of my subtle body's passing through its fibers did forever leave their mark upon its heart. Thus was my visage and countenance truly seen and known as evidence that I truly had returned.

Now, this sacred relic of my ascension and living proof of all my words and teachings must be returned to Israel, for if it is not, its protective power will begin to have a reverse effect of how it was intended, and those who guard it will truly fall. They have served their missions well, but now all does draw quickly to a close, and all things must be set right and put in their proper place for final peace to be made. If cycles are extended beyond their natural course, then great misfortune shall befall all who hinder its true ways. Thus have I shared the secret of the Shroud, and thus must it find its true home once again.

THE DEAD SEA SCROLLS

The Dead Sea Scrolls have an intelligence and consciousness all their own that does truly guide their actions and those of the men about them. The Scrolls did have an important part to play to right the errors of past ways of the church and its elders. Truly the Scrolls have already been deciphered, yet the truth they do bear would bring great men and institutions to ruin, and thus their truths have been suppressed. The followers of Brigham Young do truly have them, but a deal has been struck to keep the silence golden until the proper time.

The scandals now facing the church and its leaders are thought to be too much if the burden of the Scrolls were to be added upon it. Yet this is a grave error, for the Scrolls do wish to be known, and the longer their truth is delayed, the worse shall be the disaster. Great cities and institutions and traditions must fall and be completely destroyed before new vitality and purity might truly restore their former glory, and the longer the church does delay this process, the worse shall its fury be.

The Scrolls were written and hidden by ancient mystics of Judea who were taught and initiated by two Disciples who did have the gift to see. The brothers James and John did truly know the prophecy and included upon their endeavors to record their truths upon those Scrolls. Then the Angel Gabriel did instruct them where they were to be hidden that they would remain preserved and undisturbed until others were led to find them in these recent years. The Scrolls did call to those souls who had agreed to uncover them and bring their truths to light, and so those who do hide their truth, out of fear and mistrust in God's ways, do only make matters worse.

The Scrolls do bear forth the true meaning of the mysteries of the Second Covenant, which the church has long abused and misinterpreted to maintain its own advantage and power. It was truly known and seen that this would occur, and so the burden and task was placed with the Roaring Brothers to create the vessel that would right the ship after so many misguided years. All that the church does now face with abuse and scandal is a result of their leaders not having the courage or bravery to face the truth of the Scrolls and right their own ship. Pride truly does cometh before the fall, and there is none to blame but themselves. Thus must the power and truth of the Scrolls be heeded lest matters truly get worse.

OF SCIENCE, THE MIND, AND THE PROOF OF GOD'S EXISTENCE

It is a noble effort by modern man to use his tools of science to prove of the nature of God. It is the natural result of the furthest development of the mental body, which is truly the intent and success of this age, but alas it is also the great lesson for this time to see the limitations of that function of higher reasoning, and thus to take the step further into the unknown and by surpassing and releasing the mind to become a piece of soul awareness that does truly, consciously know of God in a way and in the nature and function of a way the mind cannot, for it is not possible for something of a lower nature and function to clearly and truly express and describe one of a higher.

God and Spirit and Unity is a greater and finer faculty and substance than that which constitutes the mind. The mental body does reside on the fourth plane or heaven of God. The knowledge and awareness truly of God does reside on the sixth, or soul plane and above, and thus the mental body does try to assert its own importance and nature by telling man that it does have the capacity to discern and know of God, but this is not true, for it can only turn its eye upward to the starry skies of its own plane and ponder at the wonders it does see above it.

A simple way to illustrate the relationship is thus: You could explain it to another by asking them to truly and accurately and precisely describe the nature and essence of a thought using only their hands. Though this they could do in a rudimentary and basic fashion, they could only begin to describe the most elementary characteristics of a thing so subtle and fine and complex as a thought within the mind.

Thus can be seen the difficulty of using the tools of a lower faculty to adequately describe a higher. And thus is it with trying to use the mind to define and prove of God. This lower faculty and function cannot be used to illustrate clearly the truth of a higher; it can only be known and experienced by each who is capable and willing and eager to know it. Thus, the melding of the two can begin to build a picture for man of the ways and means of God, and a description of its functioning and methods, but the mind can never prove of God, for it is a servant of Soul and a machine and truly has not the capabilities.

OF PROPHECY
AND THE NATURE OF TIME

The nature of prophecy and time are truly complex issues. Many times we do hear of the predictions and prognostications of seers for events upon the physical plane, but this should only be done with the greatest trepidation and hesitation, for the free will of man, which is why he is truly here, does play an unpredictable role in the timing and nature of events.

Seers and mystics and sages who are bestowed with the gift of sight can rise to a higher level and see clearly the hearts of men, and thus know truly what must eventually transpire, and in what order, but because man does have free will and a stubborn and misleading mind and does not always listen to the truth of his heart, his actions may sometimes be delayed in getting to the truth predicted and foreseen.

Time moves the same for all people, yet the individual pacing of events and occurrences within theirs and other lives is dependent on the choices they do make and the decisions they do enact with regard to important matters. Thus, the knowledge of a prophecy can often speed or slow its actual occurrence because the foreknowledge of what is to transpire can affect the actions and free will of man and thus cause the necessary chain of events and actions to be either accelerated or delayed.

The events and occurrences foreseen truly will at some point occur, for they must happen as foreseen for all balance and proper unfold-ment to transpire, but the events in time may be speeded or slowed depending on the actions and decisions of those who are to play a part. Thus, when you do receive or hear of any prophecy that does include a specific element of timing, you must not lay to great an emphasis on the exact date and time, for this is truly not something which can be foretold from the seer's position, because of the nature of man's free will.

Of Destiny and Free Will

The many events that do occur in a man's life are written in the stars. There are certain things that he has agreed to before he is born and which must transpire before he can leave the earth. These are significant matters that are written in the stars. Yet man also does have free will to make his own decisions and to follow his own true heart, and thus may he influence the ways and means that he does navigate to and experience, in better ways or worse, those experiences or persons whom he must encounter or know. Thus, it is a world of man that is governed by twin forces—on the one hand is the grand scheme and play of God and the role and purpose we have agreed to play in this life, and on the other is our own free will which does dictate the amount and degree of pain and difficulty we do encounter along the way.

A man who is in harmony with God's will and his own purpose does find that the challenges and difficulties of life melt away before him as his fears do not cause him difficulty or pain. The fearful man who does not listen to his heart or have the courage to follow its direction does find himself working at odds with God's will and grand design and beset by seemingly insurmountable problems and difficulties that never seem to end. The key to all is the ability to open the heart to love and hear clearly of its directions, and this is a gradual skill that is slowly acquired as one ventures along the path back to God.

OF THE SUCCESS OF MY MISSION

I did seek in my mission on earth to spread of the Father's teachings to many lands and peoples and places and to leave a legacy of the works of my true words and truth—that all who did come after should know truly of what I did say and could study the ways and techniques to gain of the glory of heaven. But this was not the case, for I did leave the earthly plane with no record of my true teachings for others to follow home. And so I have had to wait 2,000 years to finally share of my true heart. I did prematurely end my time nailed upon the Cross for my errors of judgment and failure to listen to those of my Line who had warned me of using my powers in public and obvious ways. And so I failed to spread my truth to the many who did seek it, and did also not leave of my words for others to return home to heaven. And thus do I consider my mission a failure though this may be difficult for many to hear and know.

MY CRUCIFIXION

Now of the Crucifixion. As I was raised aloft, I did flee the body and look with sorrow downward and saw the good man Cassius act and prevent the destruction of my temple. His act of compassion and great grace did truly fulfill the prophecy, and his spear has stood on victor's side for many a passing century. My Crucifixion was the sign of the failure of my mission. To die aloft upon the cross meant the end of all I had put forth to build and spread.

The love of God would not be heard in those far lands where I did desire to travel, and those with minds for power and gain did seize upon the weakness of my followers and create a great legacy of oppression that followed in my wake. They did not serve of my mission to teach truly of love and ascension. There have been some charitable deeds that have come of my Lineage, but by and far the whole of it has been to utter destruction. In this I did fail. Men have died in numbers as a result of misunderstandings of the teachings in my name. And many, too, have taken great steps onward to salvation from the truths that they have learned. But always must it be remembered that to kill in my name is not an act of grace or merit, yet to love one another and your brother as yourself is truly an act of grace and merit that shall lead you to heaven's gates.

Though the Cross is worshipped by many and revered as a symbol of my sacrifice and love, it is not the symbol of my mission that I would have preferred. The Cross to me does represent my failure to give of my love and truth to all who did seek it in my day, and to record for all of history and man of my true words and heart to guide them forever on the path.

The Mother Mary is the sign whom I would have preferred to see, for her loving devotion and commitment to God was truly an inspiring image for all who did know of my true heart and intentions. My mission was a failure, for more were the souls that suffered under the yoke of false teachings than were those that profited from my words and sailed ever onward. Now must be the time to set all back on course. Though many will find these words difficult to take within, they are the words of truth and my everlasting gospel.

OF THE JOURNEY OF SOUL

Each man is struggling in his own way to find a higher state of grace. The illusions that plague man on earth are great, and each must be given the space and freedom to evolve at his own pace. None has the right to interfere with the growth and development of another, and none may yet tell him of the path or place that he should be. We are each individual children of God; come here to learn the difficult lessons that temper soul to its true steel. We are being purified that we should truly know ourselves and finally arrive to seek our true place in the heavens of God. It is not a journey that lasts a single lifetime.

This is a tool of power and fear that has been used by the church to control man for all the ages past. Truly did the Eastern masters well understand this better. Many thousands of years are required, sometimes more, to bring a soul closer to perfection. However, the key to all success is love and trust in the grace of God. When you open yourself to the guidance of your heart, you shall hear God speaking through you and directing you ever onward to greater glory. There is no glory won in triumphing at the cost of another.

Of the Spear of Longinus

The Spear of Longinus was the weapon that Cassius did use to pierce of my breast and mercifully end of my suffering, that the Roman soldiers did not come and break of all my bones. When the Spear did pierce my side and touch of my blood, it did become imbued with an awesome power and might as the very essence of my nature did flow into its steel and gold and forever reside there to protect and serve whoever did bear it at their side. It did become a totem of dual powers, for it was a weapon as its nature and a servant of the dark side of the forces of the universe, but when it did touch of the pure light power that was transferred from my blood, it did become an awesome weapon that could be used for good or wrong as its wielder did see fit. And thus was the talisman created that did guide the conquering hands of the many kings of Europe, up until Hitler's time, and even to the present day in the hands of those in America who do wield of its power to protect of those mighty shores.

And of Forgiveness

Of forgiveness, I shall say this: Many are the wrongs that man does incur against his neighbor in ignorance of Divine Law, and much is the pain that is created in these works. Many are the injustices that each of you do impart upon those you do love in your imperfect understanding of my words. I must tell you this: Forgiveness is the ability to see and kindly understand the error of your neighbor as he does see and understand yours. All make best efforts to do as they do think right and proper, but different is each of us in our level of understanding. For those of greater awareness, the burden does fall to understand the ways of those less awakened, though never should anything be said of this account. 'Tis a special gift to give great love to another without the need to bring into the light the sight of greater weakness and ignorance.

Great is the grace of God to those who can allow the lesser awakened to trod peacefully along their path in error and illusion. I speak of the grave ills that are committed in my name as well. I must expand my heart and love past all known reaches to pour forth the great bounty of forgiveness to all who have committed atrocious sins in my name in the wrong thought that they did truly serve my ways. Indeed, the whole of the church must seek the forgiveness of the flock for the grievous error of their wayward indiscretions. Not all shall forgive easily, yet this is the mark of the truly blessed and the enlightened. Forgiveness must be genuine and true and of the heart, for if it is not authentic, then lo does it not accomplish its true aim—to open the heart, though often with difficulty, to a greater flow of love for all the world.

The hardness in the hearts of man was the great reason I did come here, and I shall not find rest until all have allowed the grace of love to enter into their hearts. This must occur for me to have found success and peace. Force of arms and aggression against another are the signs of fear and illusion, and the mark of the hardened heart. Tigers shall fight among themselves till fear does consume and kill them all, even to a one. Only true brothers shall stand tall and side-to-side and remain standing after all tigers have fallen.

You must learn to forgive those who trespass against you. This lesson is truly well to be heeded, for it bears forth great truth. When you find in your heart the anger rising for the actions of another, then gently call my name and look in your heart for the understanding of the cause of your aggressor's misunderstanding and ignorance of the proper course of love. Do not let yourself be a martyr, but stand strong in your defense and true in your intention. The man of pure heart and cause shall always in the end find victory and glory in the heart of heaven.

The difficult lessons that my son did learn were of the grace of forgiveness: to not draw arms or harbor ill against those who did greatly wrong us. Each man is struggling in his own way to find a higher state of grace. The illusions which plague man on earth are great, and each must be given the space and freedom to evolve at his own pace. None has the right to interfere with the growth and development of another, and none may yet tell him of the path or place that he should be. We are each individual children of God; come here to learn the difficult lessons that temper soul to its true steel.

What of Tolerance

Of tolerance, I can say this: Many different faces and many different places will all come together in coming years. There shall be a variety of man on earth like none ever witnessed. Man must learn not to fear those that appear different from him. We all seek the same home and share the same Father. Our different colors and visages bear only to the great grace and divine creativity of our Master. They are a testament to the beauty of creation that surrounds us and a thing to be celebrated.

Do not allow the differences in color or creed to bring fear into your hearts even unto visitors from far off places. There shall truly come to be seen those that are not of this world. Upon earth is all the same of this rule: that you should treat all others as if they were of your own blood, for truly all are your brothers. Man must learn to open his heart to all that he finds in his path regardless of their creed or color. Even language and custom may differ greatly in different places, but this, too, is evidence of the Father's great wisdom and eternally inspired creativity.

MY VIEWS ON CHRISTIANITY

Now, onto my legacy: I did not intend a world religion to follow in my name. My goal was to speak and share great secrets of truth and leave behind the books that shared the techniques for the great return home. Every world religion, when it becomes large enough, becomes a social organization focused on the accumulation of power and wealth and devoted to change. The true paths are concerned only with the return of man to God, for all else flows naturally as an extension and benefit from this process. I came to earth to spread a message of love and to open man's hearts to God. That there was a monstrous organization that resulted was not my intention or doing.

OF THE NICENE CREED

Of the Nicene Creed, I say this: that the code was not pure and did not speak of truth. Mary was the blessed one who held me closely to her and brought me forth that I should be able to well survive the winter. The church has made my death a disgrace and has held the greatest sign of my failure as a symbol of non-hope. These false teachings shall not remain in my name. The Mother Mary was the symbol who rightly did represent me, and it must quickly be returned to honor her great memory. Power and fear are the legend of the Cross, and this must be erased from all memory. My message and mission was of hope and love, not of Roman treachery.

OF MY SON BENJAMIN

Of my great son Benjamin, I can say this: that truly did Mary Magdalene have a deep and special place within my heart, and deeply did I love and care for her. She truly knew me as no other, and I was honored to have her bear my son. It was a clean conception and birth with no major complications, and Benjamin was a beautiful boy who had a pure and noble heart. We did decide for his safety to place him with a noble family and did send him to be raised by the Martels. They were a great and noble line, and I did know even then that my son would create the Order of the Knights of the Grail to protect man from the darkness while I would be gone. He did do his job well, and made his father proud, and more will be said of this later.

How the Disciples Were Chosen

Of the Disciples, I can say this: that they were all selected for the brilliant shine of their hearts, and for their dedication to the truth. Each had his own foibles and qualities that made him proper for his specific role. Within each group of twelve there exists a certain dynamic that must be in place for success to be realized. As with the twelve months of a year, so do the dispositions of different men comprise the fullness of all experience to create a complete and functioning whole. Yet care must be taken by the sun to keep each planet and month in its proper balance, lest a change in the good path of any should create chaos for the whole.

Truly did I well select those who would best serve my great cause, but by my own errors did I create imbalances that led to our ultimate fall. I did not give enough care to my actions, and so the delicate nature of each man was thrown out of balance and his predisposition to the strengths that he did possess was weakened and left exposed. I was not careful with my actions, and the miracles and cures that I did perform created an imbalance of energy within the heavens.

Those who were closest to me did not have sufficient training and strength to remain balanced in the face of such great change. The flux and flow of the currents of the universe did throw them from their good and balanced paths and the harmony of our union was put asunder. There can be no blame placed on any but me, for it was my ignorance of the Divine Laws that caused their utter destruction. Had I listened better to the warning of my Brothers, I should have fared more carefully along the narrow path.

Of each individually, I can say this: James was picked for his bravery and truth in the face of treachery. Judas for his fear of his own self which created a deep mistrust of all not completely dedicated to the path, for he was well selected to see into the hearts of others and see of the weaknesses there. Bartholomew was a noble soul who did see deeply into all matters and did have a great wisdom and knowledge of God that did serve as an inspiring example to all others. John the Baptist, though not one of my Disciples, was stout of limb and heart and knew of many good ways to attract followers. Peter, too, had a fine way and cheerful countenance and was well able to understand and move the hearts of a great crowd. Matthew was a gentle soul whose knowledge of music and the mysteries of soul did bring all to his gentle loving ways. John was a builder and shaper of the hearts of men and could open even the hardest of souls unto their own true being. James, his brother, was the son of every man and did well know the way into the common heart—his words and song did speak to all that we did desire to draw near.

Of the rest, I will say more later. Each had his own strength and particular skill that endeared him to our number, and each had his own flaw that was balanced within our hearts.

Of the Disciples, I can say this: Many were there who did desire to come and sit by my side, and many did disagree with whom I did select, yet there was a logic and reason. The inner eyes do truly see beyond the mind or reason. I did know the heart of each who sat beside me and did value all that he brought to our efforts.

There is a time though, that all of best-laid plans are put asunder, when laws that are to remain untouched do get badly broken. The Disciples did their very best to remain strong and above the waves of my actions, yet they had not the sight nor training to understand or know what must be done. I was not able to teach them quickly enough all that they did need to know.

At our Last Supper, I did tell them all of my rhyme and reason and of what end I was truly to come. Then they partook of my flesh and blood that my spirit would remain inside and work through them. This was my final act of love for those great souls that I had failed. They gave me of their hearts and best efforts and I was unable to carry them truly onward to glory and great fame.

A FAREWELL TO LOVED ONES

When those who we hold dear do find their earthly days finally come to an end, it can be a difficult moment as the pain of loss does sweep within our hearts and engulf us with our tears. And though the passing to the other side is merely a change of state and location, for the soul is everlasting, it is often an occurrence that does leave us seeking words to ease the pain of our loss.

I do give this prayer to all who have lost of one they did hold dear to ease the passage on.

PRAYER FOR THE DYING

When death does knock upon the door, and the love of hearts is fleeting,
Then turn your ear unto my heart and listen for me truly.

My name with love shall open wide the great door of pain and pining,
And you shall stride without any fear, through it and quickly to me.

When you seek to hear my voice and heart amongst the clatter,
Then call my name and I shall be, my heart within the matter.

My love for you does know no bounds, and I shall always be there.
When you are lost, just sing for me, and I shall always be there.

I shall be here waiting for all who say my name with love and affection in grief and in pain at the passing of those they do love. These are the words to heal my young flock in all their pains.

BAPTISMAL FOR CHILDREN

The children of the world are dearest to my heart, for they have yet to suffer of the harsh lessons and trials of the experiences of life and living, and the difficult journey home to God. And so I do bless their innocence and gentle laughter and loving nature with this baptismal prayer that it should provide them with my love and protection as they do grow and mature and begin to set forth upon their own true path back to God.

For the children I do say this:

SONG OF BAPTISM FOR THE CHILDREN

You come to me that you might know the greatness of my glory,
Yet truly shall I give to you a gift of greater loving.

When the new child does come to seek the water of most holy,
Then touch his head and think of me, and I shall come and fill thee.

The rites of love run deep within the hearts of all that surround thee,
And when my name is spoken thus, I shall enter and never leave thee.

My heart runs deep within the lands, and goes to all that need me,
Just look for me and I do come, if you shall ever need me.

This is the song of baptism for the children. You have heard me truly.

AND WHAT OF FALSE TEACHERS

There is a need in these writings to speak to the heart of all that has been lost by man. There is a great deal of love that has been given to all upon the earth, yet they do not know what they truly have received. They cannot see or know the miracles of their own faith and knowledge of God. I must speak to you of the truth of individual knowledge of God that my flock might not be led astray by conjurers and magicians. There is much that can be said of the true knowledge of God, but for each man it is truly an individual thing.

For the masses to know, however, that what they do experience is real, I must say this: When you do say my or any other holy name in quiet reflection, there must come to you some evidence of perfection that arises from without your own mind. Though it may take some time to reach this state where this may occur, this is truly the test of all that is real. When your heart is truly opened, then any real master may be able to come to you in your quiet and make himself known to you. If your teacher is not able to speak to you thusly, then you have embarked upon a false teaching and not a true path home to God.

Many are there who promise everlasting life to the faithful, and many are the charlatans who do take the hard-earned money of the poor. This is the test of supreme love that I do give them. Faith only must be used as a tool to embark upon the journey. If in your heart, and after a good time, you have not truly seen or heard the voice of the Master, then you truly have been deceived. Thus will all know that they are truly embarked upon the true path back to God. In dreams as well may the Master's voice be heard or face seen, but some genuine occurrence must take place. Do not put your faith or trust in false masters who cannot truly lead you upon the path back to the Father.

Of false prophets, I may say this: The lands are now full with those who claim to have divine right. This is truly a lie, for few are there who truly know the true Word of God. The prophets vanish from the earth, and the few who do remain the people do not see or acknowledge.

When the people do seek for confirmation of their spiritual leaders, they must remember this: God is a living, alive, and active, conscious, presence, and any who does not have this from their teacher is truly being well-deceived. Having God in your life is like having a good friend you may always turn to. Be vigilant in your thoughts, and do not give your heart readily to all who would seek it. The trust in a teacher is a sacred thing, and he must be held to the highest standard. Do not be afraid to seek another if he should truly not be giving you what your heart does truly desire.

Man has seen and known and heard of many coming saviors. From East and West and North and South, they have come from all the corners. Many have there been who have come before and after with messages of truth and brotherly love. Mine was a special message for those times and for that place did greatly differ from all others. For I was the One to bring to those peoples and cultures the voice of love and compassion and forgiveness that had been heard in other places but never before by these ears.

Love is all there is in this universe that can lead to the true happiness and a return home. None of all the illusions may take a man even a hair's breadth closer to God than what already lies locked within his own heart. He must learn well to listen to what his heart tells him. It has a powerful wisdom all its own that far surpasses that of the mind.

When the questions arise in the mind of man as to what is the proper direction, he must close his eyes and quietly say my name and enter into reflection. If his desire is pure and he does yearn to find the right direction, then all my love shall come to him, for his passionate and brave true mention. I am here still to help those that will open their hearts to me, but I shall brook no slander or ill use of my name for the desecration of love or any symbols. I am a teacher of the path of love, and that is all there is. Do not use my name to justify fearful actions.

AND OF REINCARNATION

We are each individual children of God who come here to learn the difficult lessons that temper soul to its true steel. We are being purified that we should truly know ourselves and finally arrive to seek our true place in the heavens of God. It is not a journey that lasts a single lifetime. This is a tool of power and fear that has been used by the church to control man for all the ages past.

Truly did the Eastern masters well understand this better. Many thousands of years are required, sometimes more, to bring a soul closer to perfection. However, the key to all success is love and trust in the grace of God. When you open yourself to the guidance of your heart, you shall hear God speaking through you and directing you ever onward to greater glory. There is no glory won in triumphing at the cost of another.

AND OF HOLY UNION

For those entering into the holy vow of marriage, I do say this: The union of man and wife is a sacred thing and not to be taken lightly, though not for all time may this union truly be. As a man and woman develop together, there may come a time that they do need to part to continue on their own path. The road of spiritual growth does not always follow along the same tracks for each soul. When this is the case, then this man and woman who do truly love each other with only goodwill and support will not try to hold one another back out of fear or any other need.

It is often the case that they shall return to each other's side as complete and whole beings after having had some time to develop on their own. In all cases, the most important thing is the mutual respect and love and the sanctity of the right of each person to make their own choices. No man does own or possess his wife or have any right to control her or to tell her what to do. Each in the marriage shall support and love the other and aid in their growth and development in any manner possible. When one is weaker than the other, then there can be created an imbalance that does truly lead to poor ends.

OF MARRIAGE AND PARTNERS

Marriage is an institution of man, but blessed by God, and was originally conceived as a means of stabilizing disruptive social forces during earlier barbaric times when man was less civilized in his treatment of his fellow brother and of women. It was seen by the ruling fathers of those early times that an institution was needed to protect man from his neighbors and bind him to the protection of women and children, and so marriage was conceived of as a good answer and solution. The church did, as a matter of convenience, bless and support these unions as it was commonly done, but it was never a divine rule of law or practice of what sex should commit to the other. It was merely a means of stabilizing society in those tumultuous and difficult times.

Today, things have changed and marriage is a different matter. However, any commitment of partnership that does promote a loving and caring relationship of one to another and does create a family vehicle to support each other's endeavors and desires to return back home to God and to live and learn and teach of his Divine Laws is a partnership and marriage that should be sanctioned and blessed by the church, for souls are souls and are both male and female, and neither male nor female, and marriage is merely the commitment of two souls who have found in one another a loving similitude that has caused them to desire to share of each other's lives, and none may rightfully stand in the way of two who do wish to commit to each other in this manner. Thus must all things and customs evolve to fit the changing needs of those who they do serve. And so must the institution of marriage evolve to fit the changing needs of man and his society as he does continue to evolve and unfold.

PRAYER FOR THE HOLY UNION OF TWO

When two do come to find great love, in the service of each other,
Then as their friend and one great love, let nothing put them asunder.

The love of God does know no bounds, and truly does he give it,
To all who seek to give their hearts, and never shall they break it.

When you do come upon the earth, and God does walk between you,
Then fear not for his love being lost, for I shall never leave you.

One love above, and so below, and this is all there is,
For none may be without the touch of a heart that is truly awakened.

This shall be the prayer for the consecration of marriage.

OF INTERCESSION
AND THE PRIESTHOOD AND CLERGY

The roles of priests and the clergy is to instruct of my flock on the techniques and ways of practice and living that they might come to each know God for themselves. Each of us does have the capability and the right as soul to hear of God's true voice with our own hearts and ears and to listen to HIS directions and guidance in making the decisions and learning the lessons of life and Divine Law.

The priesthood and clergy do have no monopoly on the ear and heart of God or Christ. They are merely schooled in the ways of living and the techniques for knowing of God, and it is their duty of service to my name and to the Father to do all within their powers to show the flock the way to God's heart that each person might have his or her own relationship and experience with God to guide him or her truly upon the path of life.

It is not the single domain of any to bear the only voice of God and any who do say so seek only of their own power and control at the expense and freedom of those who do trust, and thus do they violate the free will and purpose of God and will be held to answer for their actions. This is the proper role of the priests and clergy as teachers and guides, but nothing more.

OF PRIESTLY VOWS

Now, onto the sacrament for the brothers and sisters. To the brothers and sisters of the quiet life, I do say this prayer:

A PRAYER FOR QUIET BROTHERS AND SISTERS

When you are called by your great King, to enter into His service,
Then it is well to hear these words, and go within quite wordless.

The life you choose does honor Him, and truly He is joyful,
To know that all your heart will fill, with love for all the people.

When you are called to sally forth, and share good works and wishes,
Then think of me, and I shall come, to help relieve all burdens.

The mission of God is one of love, and only some are called thus,
For service still builds love and trust, for the One who always serves us.

This shall be the prayer for the brothers. For the sisters, I do say this same prayer, for there is no great difference in mine eyes for either of those. Service in the love of God is a mighty calling, and only the noble and pure of heart shall indeed find solace and greatness in its quietude and loneliness. When there is a need to come into contact with others, this seclusion should be broken that the inspiration and word of God and hope might be carried forth when the messenger does feel that he is ready. Those of the quieter cloth indeed are greatly blessed, for they toil tirelessly without fame or glory, and I shall always watch closely over all who do bear forth with love in their hearts and my name on their lips.

OF JESUS' MESSAGE
TO JOHN THE BAPTIST

John was a great teacher until his dying day, though after our number did swell and begin to gain many followers, he did begin to slow down. He did not want to interfere with the great efforts of importance that he knew we did carry forth. When he was close to death at the hand of Herod the ruler, I did say to him a simple message of love and hope that he had given of his great heart to serve of God's great children, and now they did send him home. I, too, would one day join him, for my time I knew would come.

When John did read these words, he did know in his heart that the great prophecy would be fulfilled, and I was the One true teacher. The Essenes had a long and ancient belief that the One true Son of God would be sent to man but would be rejected and returned home to the Father while nailed to a Cross. Thus did I show to him that though not an Essene, I had foreseen my future and did know truly of my own end. This did give him the sign that he did seek, and he did come unto my heart before at last he died.

OF THE MISSIONARY TRADITION

Of the missionary tradition, I can say this: that the Word of God is well to be spread to those dark corners where it is truly needed, but participation in its teachings and in the conversion to its ways is only to be a voluntary undertaking by the seeker. No missionary of my name or member of my flock shall ever, by force or word or mind or action, push the truth of my teachings or words on another, for to do so is a gross violation of Divine Law.

Each man or woman has the true and proper right to select his own path and religion and way of believing, and there is no man or any other who does have the right to attempt to change his views or selection by any matter of force. There are many different paths of truth upon this earth—indeed one each to fit each and every level of consciousness and development, and it is to each individual soul to find that one which is appropriate for him and for his level of learning. Thus will some come to my teachings, and thus will some leave, and this freedom of choice truly must be respected else Divine Law should be violated and great burden of cause and effect and further pain incurred.

CLOSING TO SCRIPTURES

These are the words of my truth, and the Scriptures I have given of my heart to the Scribe as my gift of love and hope to all who do seek of heaven. There have been many years of pain and loss and misguided action by those who do wield and abuse of my name. But now I have finally come again to be heard truly and right of all previous wrongs. Now, none do have of any reason or excuse not to know of my true heart and intent and purpose in my mission upon the earth. And all who do continue to take false steps and actions and who do violate the Laws of God in my name shall be called to account for their actions, and no quarter or forgiveness shall be given to those who do knowingly go against my will and wishes.

For many long years have I answered and pleaded for those who did commit great sins out of ignorance and errors of understanding of my ways. But no longer shall this be the case, for the Scribe has brought to you the truth of my heart and you are well-advised to heed of my words and study the truths and keys here given that you might proceed with haste and certain success upon the narrow center path back to God.

And so, I do give you the heart of my truth and love, for I do love all of my flock dearly and long to greet you at the home of our Father in heaven at the end of your long journey. Look well to the hearts of the Disciples and my family, for they do bear great wisdom and truth as well to aid you on the path.

My blessings and love to you always.

Amen.

CHAPTER TWO

THE GOSPEL OF THE TWELVE DISCIPLES

INTRODUCTION

JESUS: My twelve Disciples were those who sat about me and learned of my heart and all that I did teach and share. It was their true and solemn duty to take my words and spread them to all hearts that sought the truth of God. Though they did well serve my mission and aid of my great cause, their words and true hearts have lost certain meaning and understanding with all the passing years. While many of their words are captured in the Bible and other places, this is only part of the truth of their understanding. They have come now to complete of their teachings and share of their true hearts that all might finally know of their learnings and love and that they might complete of their duties and move on to other realms. Thus does now follow the true words of my Disciples, as I did teach to them the great wonders of God and they did fulfill of their duties and mission.

THE GOSPEL
ACCORDING
TO PETER

OF LOVE

Of love between the sexes, I can say this: that there does exist
between two who truly love each other an inalienable right to the
expression and true respect and protection of that love, and no man
may rend asunder what God does truly put together. However, this
is not to say that one may own the other, for the love is based on mutual
respect, love, and support of the other's feelings and needs. The
covenant of love is to see the best grow and flourish in each individual—
that each should progress rapidly and steadily on the great path back
to God. The man and woman or partner must give the love and
support that the other does need and require to face the lessons of Spirit
that are given for each to overcome. Thus does the partner in the
relationship each become an instrument of divine will and love in
aiding the other onward.

Of love within the family, I can say this: that the parents of the child
have a true duty and obligation to steer their young charge successfully
upon the winding and rocky path of life. At times, the child will not
like, understand, or appreciate the role that the parent does truly play.
But as the parent does guide the child in his decisions, it is always with
the intent of teaching those skills and rules of Divine Law that shall
enable the child to quickly learn all important lessons and proceed with
haste and success on his true road home. Though those decisions are
often difficult, the child is well to respect his elders until he does come
of age to truly make all his own decisions. Any parent who does shirk

in his duty to the protection of his children shall earn many more lives of pain and suffering on the wheel of reincarnation.

Of love between strangers, I can say this: that each should treat another as if he were one of his own family. Even those of other races, colors, and cultures do truly share the same heritage of God and do deserve the respect and love that one would show their own family.

DIVINE LAW

My law of God that must not be violated pertains specifically to women and children, as they are those who do need most greatly of God's protection. I do especially abide the law of protection for those who have none. Though this is not a specific Divine Law, it is a sacred principle that must be remembered when each and every soul does go about his day and make good and right decisions.

MORALITY

Of morality, I will say this: that all actions for good or bad may be judged by these few laws. First, does it violate the sanctity of personal freedom of choice and direction of another? Second, does it violate the free will of worship of the God of their choosing? And last, does it inter-fere with the Soul's progress back home to the eternal heavens? These are the measures by which all actions may be accounted.

MY LIFE MISSION

I did know that it was my mission to serve by the Christ's side when there did appear to me a vision of the Angel Gabriel, and he did direct me where to find the Christ and what was to be my role. I did trust him completely, and quickly to His side did I go.

THE LAST SUPPER

At the Last Supper, the Christ did tell us of what was to happen, and we did share of His blood and body. Then He held us in a close circle and spoke the sacred words that did seal our love and His together for all time. We did understand beyond a shadow of a doubt what must transpire and why, and though we were greatly saddened did serve the Father's wishes to reclaim HIS only begotten Son. Thus did we watch Him go with His chains and crown of thorns to make the ultimate sacrifice for the great love of man that He did bear within His heart.

OF MY BETRAYAL

Truly did we serve the Christ King well, and many were the long nights of fear and isolation. We did know all that was to transpire and even of our own role in it, for He had told us so. He truly knew of our hearts before even the deed was done and especially did He select us for what He knew that we would truly do. The hearts of men hold no secrets for those with open eyes.

When the soldiers did find me that night upon the open road and bring me to my knees, I did beg them of their mercy. But I was weak and the terrible pain and fear in my heart drove me to my betrayal. I did not know that I was capable of such a great fear or loss of love for the One whom I had truly sworn to protect always. When the Christ did find out what I had done, He held me close with my head upon His heart and bid me not to worry. He had truly known what I would do, and how all would transpire. The Christ had seen ahead, and knew how all plans must be achieved, and His great love for me was not tainted by the weakness of my deed.

MY CONVERSATION WITH PAUL OF TARSUS

I did tell Paul truly of what was the nature and ways of my experiences within the Christ's great Circle. I did say to him that God had truly become a living, breathing, real thing to me; that I could feel in my life and in my heart in each and every moment; and that I had truly seen of the miracles and love of Christ and His ability to know and do things no man before had ever been able to achieve. Thus did I share with him of my heart and truest feelings and bid him to join our number. He did thank me truthfully, and come within our circle that he, too, might experience of the great joy and happiness that we did truly know.

MY RELATIONSHIP TO MARK

Of Mark, I can say this: that he was a true friend and fellow teacher of the great ways of the Christ. We did travel far and wide to bring his great words of love and truth for all who would hear and listen. Mark truly did make all successes possible, for he was an earnest and eager seeker and did well remember all that had been said and done. He did carry us onward always at the end of long days and dusty roads. When I did begin to tire and look about in despair, 'twas always he who did come forth to find an answer to our prayers. Mark was that great and true soul who truly did make all my journeys and successes possible, for dedicated was he to our cause, noble of heart, stout of limb and quick of mind. Without his true and noble efforts, all would have fallen to the wayside.

We did travel widely across the seas to Cairo, to the North, the East and beyond to what is now France and Spain. And as we did cross the lands and seas, we did share the teachings of Christ to all who would listen and were interested. In some fair lands, we were received with love and open arms and hearts—in others with fear and worry and scorn. But it mattered not how they did greet us, for we gave them of our love and by our example did show them an alternative way of seeing the world and believing in the cause and true matter of human nature. We were chased by kings and priests of other races and faiths, cast out by unbelievers, and shouted down and stoned when we did teach of truth that others did not want to be known. And so with Mark at my side for support and assistance, we did go forth to all the lands and do of our true work.

Two things I do well remember were these I do tell now. First, in Mycenae, upon the shores of that fair city where we did come upon a distraught maiden weeping by the sea. In her arms, she held the body of her love who had drowned in the stormy seas. He was a fisherman and a lad of noble features, and it did tear upon my heart to see one so young and in so much grief. Mark did beg me heal him, and so I did perform the secret technique. After I had completed and the life of him had returned, then we did quickly continue on our way after making them truly swear to never say a word.

Of the other incident, there is this: that as we gained the city, we did see by the side of the road a broken and upturned cart with several bloodied peasants lying by its side. They had been misplaced when the Roman legions had forced them from the road. I did feel this was as good a time as any to add them to our cause, and so I did go forth and heal them and quickly return them on their way. These two things did I truly do and experience.

THE RESURRECTION
OF MY MASTER

When Jesus came again arisen and before me stood and smiled, I did lay my hands upon Him and see that He was real. Of flesh and blood He did stand before me, as real as any other man, and He did speak and tell me of what must next transpire for Him to finally transcend. The Christ did wish all his Disciples to know that He had not left them and would always be by their side, that there was life in the ever after, and the Father would greet them there. That we all did have great merit, and great missions to fulfill, and that although he had failed, He knew we would succeed, for all now rested upon our shoulders. Then He did say that He was to go and see of Mary the Mother, and the others who did truly need to hear of His heart one final time. And then He did go and was gone before my very eyes. This I do recall and truly remember of His resurrection.

OF MIRACLES I PERFORMED
IN MY MASTER'S NAME

Of the cripple at the gate, there is this: I came upon the temple to say my prayers and offerings to those who did reside and saw the wretched one set before my way, broken and sprawled upon the stairs. He had a gentle countenance, though I could well not see his face, and he smiled as I passed by him, and I could feel his grace. For one who had so little to be able to give to me so much did well remind me of the teachings of the Risen Teacher, and so I did return to the cripple at the gate and give to him the sacred techniques that the Christ had taught us and returned him to his feet.

Of the paralytic at Lydda, there is another tale. I had traveled to Lydda to seek of matters there and did come across a paralyzed girl stricken from the face below and unable to move or even smile. I did gently take her head in my hands and look into her eyes and did truly see and know of what was the past life issue arisen in her present form to make her thus. Silently I did ask her if she would accept an alternative form of penance. And as she did agree, I did shift her payment to an area of service that she truly could perform. She did commit her life to Christ and the service of his teachings to the poor, and thus was her affliction lifted as long as she did keep her word. Thus was the paralytic at Lydda transformed.

THE CENTURION CORNELIUS

Cornelius was a noble soldier, and one of the Centurion Guards, and he often did find our Brothers' teaching in his areas of responsibility. Many times did he berate us and roughly send on our way, but we did always return and with hearts of love and compassion did firmly stand our ground and offer him another way. Thus, after much time and patience—the course of nearly a year—did he truly come to be able to hear of our hearts and listen to what we did say. Finally, he did bid us come one night to his home, and there did he have us baptize his family into the Master's way. It was a joyous occasion and an event that does truly linger ever on my heart.

RAISING THE DEAD

I did truly raise the woman Dorcas who lived in that fair city of Joppa. There was a dire and grave circumstance that did lead me to commit this single act, for I was loathe to ever perform this service on one whose time had truly come to go, but this was an exceptional case. The woman did have a family of three young sons and a girl who had not a father to look after and protect them and no other relatives to which to turn for succor or support. I found them all in the street, squalling upon their dead young mother's breast. A crowd did gather round but showed no compassion or pity, for Dorcas had been of ill repute and out of favor with the villagers.

I did bid Mark to help me carry her to a private place and after much consternation and indecision did decide to return her to her shell. As I quietly went within and Mark did stand over me, I performed the sacred technique and returned the grateful mother to her sons. Those who later did see her walking did ask what had occurred, but I carefully had told her to say it was only a minor illness that had taken her momentarily to other realms. Thus was she healed and returned and none was any the wiser.

Of importance it is to note also that she had been the daughter of a noble man of the town, and when he did finally agree to see her and heard of what had truly transpired, he did bid us to come and sit with him and share his food and wine. And thus did we find shelter and support for our teachings in that small town.

My Relationship with Paul of Tarsus

Paul and I did truly see differently on matters of the Christ as it related to Greece and Rome. Paul did believe that although the Christ was dead and gone that His truth and words could be intuited and heard by any man regardless of his station and level of training and development in the truths and works of God. I did truly disagree and did say that a man must have the knowledge and training and initiations to be able to declare himself a vessel and voice of the Christ, for what Paul did say and attribute to our Master were not things He had ever said.

Paul did not believe me and said they had been truly given to him, and I was not one to be able to know what he had been truly told by the dead Christ. Thus did we always bicker, and our roads did begin to diverge. Paul was a jolly fellow and popular with the common man, and it was important, he did feel, to his mission that his words forever would endure. And thus did he himself end upon a cross and crucified for his teachings.

MY MESSAGE TO TODAY'S FLOCK

JESUS: When I and the Disciples did pass to the heavenly realms, we did not abandon our duties or those we do love on earth. There is a true saying "on earth is it so above" and this does allow us the ability to see and observe of what does daily occur in the lives of man. So it is with understanding and hearts of compassion and love that we do see of modern happenings and share of our true hearts to aid those who still toil and strive in the worlds below.

PETER: The Roman Catholics of this day must truly know and remember that only the words of those who were known to and initiated by the Christ do well reflect the holy truth of His teachings. All other words may provide succor and warmth, but they must always be remembered for the words of another and must therefore be considered as possibly being false, for they carry not the absolute weight of truth that the Christ did confer upon His direct Disciples.

My solution for the flock today is this: to carefully read upon the words that this holy Scribe has written, and reflect upon those of the Disciples, and find in each and everyone of their true hearts what they do find to be the real truth of the matter.

My Final Days

I did know before I did return to Rome that I would find myself truly upon a cross such as the Christ had done, but I did also know that this was to be my destiny and way—as is the fate of many true light bringers—to end painfully at the hands of those who they do love most. And so I did return with a heavy heart to bravely bear my fate. I did well remember Jesus' example, and this did give me great strength as I carried my burden upon the streets and through the jeering crowds. I did arrive and was arrested as a conspirator against the Roman power and was sentenced to death by crucifixion without a hearing in my defense. So great was the Romans' fear—now that they had killed the Risen Christ—that they did hope that by truly killing all his remaining Disciples and teachers that they might truly put their hearts at ease.

Yet this was to prove their biggest mistake, for the public spectacle of so many good souls bravely bearing to their horrible deaths did only serve to further strengthen the people's growing faith. And so I did commend myself to the Father with this simple prayer:

Father, I do seek YOU now,
In this my final moment.

I have long carried on YOUR works,
And done your noble deeds.

My road has been long,
But now has ended.

And I do truly beg YOU,
Not to close YOUR heart.

Thus did I beseech HIS love and protection and was told that truly I would be saved. And as I was raised aloft was gently slipped from the body and felt no hurt or pain. I did never return to my shell after that point though the lingering lower bodies did give the appearance of life for some time after.

BEWARE FALSE TEACHERS

As we did wander wide and far to gather earnest students, we did come upon many who did claim to also be teachers of the Christ. I did expose many charlatans by this simple test. When one does claim to be a messenger or teacher from Christ, the test given by a true Disciple is this: to close the eyes and ask him to truly repeat the words that the Christ did share to bind our hearts during the final Supper, for only those who were truly there or were inducted or initiated later by one of our Circle would truly know those words. And thus did I expose all false teachers for what they truly were and warned the common people to take care in what they did believe.

For the common man, the rule I did give them to tell of false teachers was this: that a real teacher of Christ would be able to take the student within and through the techniques and power open his heart to the love and power of the Christ such that there would be no question as to whether it all was true. If the teacher is not able to do this—to give this experience to the seeker—then he is truly a false teacher and not to be trusted.

To the flock today, I do say this: that many do abound that claim to have the ear of Christ and His true teachings. I can say only this— that unless his words and deeds and teachings do open within your heart a door to greater love and wisdom and learning, then truly he is not what he claims. It is to each an individual decision and one each must truly make, but a true Master and teacher may be known and seen by the feelings that he is able to open honestly in your heart.

THE GOSPEL
ACCORDING
TO ANDREW

OF LOVE

Of the love between partners, I can say this: that the love born of man's heart is the same as that of God for HIS children but of a far lesser degree of intensity. The love between two who do truly cherish each other is that same feeling that God does share for all HIS lost flock. It is a gift to man to teach him of what truly the word "love" does mean and what is the frequency of its emotion. Love is that sacred feeling that is the key to all the heavens, and none shall ascend forever to the heights of glory without it fully in their hearts. Thus, when two are joined in a state of constant commitment, then is a love created and sustained that does teach them of the true nature of God and help to guide them on the path home.

Of love within the family, I can say this: that the love between children or siblings can often be an affair of convenience for the resolution of past life issues, and all familial relationships should be properly weighed with this in mind. It is not always true and necessary to remain within or committed to the house once the issues and lessons have been resolved. Thus, it is the responsibility of the parent to watch over the young children until they have come of age to well make their own decisions, but the family is not a thing to be cried for or lamented if the time has truly come when its value has run its course. It is to some degree a social institution, but the time of its central importance in the stability of society has long since past.

Of love between strangers, I do say this: that often we do come upon a stranger who does seem in some way near or familiar. Often, this is a case of a lost love or friend from some past life returned to collect or pay a debt, or renew a bond of mutual love and support. One would do well to learn how to tell the difference, but no matter what the case, each new person whom we do meet on our journeys should be met and granted detached goodwill and respect for the sanctity of their own ways and customs.

DIVINE LAW

The Christ does speak all truth, but I shall add a principle that truly should not be ignored. That when one does deal with another at a distance, or behind the veil of intermediaries, as in negotiations or lawyers or business, he is still truly bound by the same laws that do apply to him directly, for the purpose and intent of his action does truly have the same consequence through another as if it were done by him directly. Indeed, the magnitude of the error is even magnified because of the involvement of another who is not in any way specifically related to the events at hand. Thus, you may not shirk your true and proper duty by hiding behind the skirts of another.

OF MORALITY

Of morality, this can now be said: There are laws of God and laws of man, and never should social custom be confused with Divine Law. It is the responsibility of each and every soul to know, understand, and obey all Divine Laws at all times regardless of what the dictates and customs of society do say. The Christ was a true Savior because He would brook no interference in the rights or ways of others in accordance with the laws of God, and this must truly be the measure.

My Life Mission

I did know that I was to serve by His side when I did first look upon Him and saw within my heart a great white glow of burning love such as I had never felt before. Thus did I know that truly was I to be His loving servant forever.

Two Memorable Experiences with Beasts and Exorcism

I was placed in the pit of lions for spreading the Gospel of Christ. It was a much-feared message of love in a land strongly ruled by power and fear. The rulers did know truly that if their people did know of an alternative way to view each other and their lives, then all good systems and order would be truly forfeit. I was given a warning and asked to stop my ways, but I could not shirk my duties, and so was sent to be slain.

When I was cast into the pit and the hungry beasts did come to me, I did force all fear from my body and gently repeated the Master's name. Then I did imagine a great beam of light emanating from my heart and going truly to connect with the heart of each great beast and in this way did tell them that I truly meant them no harm. And so they did come and lay near me, and the Romans did know that I was protected by God, and so were afraid and truly did let me go.

Of the exorcism, this is a true tale and one that I seldom tell, for it was a deed that created more troubles than the benefit was truly worth: I was called to see a child who was feverish and moaning and thrashing about, and when I did peer at her could see the darkness that did surround and possess her. I did use the sacred techniques of Jesus to bring her into the light and did chant the sacred words he had given to bring greater light where there is darkness. The child did fall limp as the great evil did leave her body, but the ignorant family did now think that this was my deed. I did try to explain that I had truly done nothing and only helped the light to do its own work.

The news of this occurrence did spread quickly through the village. And I was beset with seekers, all wishing of the same treatment and so were all possessed of seeing and receiving miracles, and none any longer cared to hear the teachings, or learn how to heal themselves. Thus did my experience with exorcism go.

As Patron Saint of Scotland

Of Scotland and my patronage, the true words and history are this: Scotland is a land beset by troubles and strife, and this is in large part due to the sacred relics spread throughout its lands. The bodies of saints and their possessions have long been strewn about in an attempt to spread their protection. Now the time has come for this to all end. I have given what protection I could to the Scottish people. But they are truly ignorant of and do well and regularly flaunt Divine Law and even one such as I cannot bend the Law of God to suit my whimsies. As time has passed and many have moved on to other duties, so have I begun to spread my attentions elsewhere.

I did truly appear before Hungus as the patron of that land and aid him in his battle to defeat the invading horde. Hungus was a king who I did truly protect for his stout heart and wisdom, and knowledge and adherence to Divine Law. Though he was an imperfect man, he did do great deeds, and I did aid him when I could.

THE LAST SUPPER

At the Last Supper, we were all assembled and in a somber mood, yet the Christ did feed us of his blood and body and sealed our love and devotion within him. He was not afraid, yet knew what must transpire and bade us be brave and strong and continue on our ways.

WHY I WAS CHOSEN BY THE MASTER

The Christ did truly select me that I was of a good and proper standing with all the merchants of our time, and the Christ did well know that He would need the wisdom and funds of those with power to accomplish His great works. I was to use my connections and influence to bring to Him those who did wield great power and did need of His teachings most. Thus did I set out to aid Him in his great cause, but it was not to be. After He had died and gone, we did try to continue His great works, but we did not succeed.

MY FONDEST MEMORY

My fondest memory was of the time that He did truly entertain a group of the wisest powerful business leaders. They did speak to Him of their great concerns of His words and actions. He turned to them after they had all spoke and gently soothed their hearts. His was a matter of love and truth, and He cared not for business matters—only that all were treated with good intentions and fairness. The circle gathered did like His words and enjoy good conversation, and then all did part and go safely on their way. This I do remember well and truly.

OF TRAVEL TO OTHER PLACES

Myself and all the others did scatter to the four winds after the Christ was buried, for there was no safe place for us any longer there. I did go with Peter to many strange and foreign lands, and there did we spread the Christ's teaching to all who would listen and care. We did go to Greece, Mycenae, Thessalonica, Egypt, the Nile Lands, and parts of Northern Africa as we did do His great work. Before when He was still walking, He did truly desire to keep us near until He was sure we all had been properly trained to well represent his teachings. We did go to places within the city to practice our words and deeds. But after He was gone, there was no more to be practiced, and we did truly leave.

MY CRUCIFIXION

Of the proconsul, I can say this: that when my time had come and I had traveled far and wide, I did no longer have any desire to continue on my path. My brothers were few in number and all had gone their ways, and so I did decide that this was a timely and good way to depart, and thus did I refuse his generous offer to kindly save my life.

When I did near the final hour, I did do as Jesus had taught: to commend my body and soul to the Father that I might be protected as I crossed to the other side. Thus did I pray in the Christ's name that the Father might answer my prayers and greet me at the doorstep. And this was truly the case, for as I did come close upon the threshold, HE did help me slip the body, and enter HIS warm embrace, and did gently lead me to my new home upon the other side.

THE GOSPEL ACCORDING TO JAMES

OF LOVE

Of love between two, I can say this: that the love that flows from one heart to another is truly of the one same stuff that is the fabric of God. HE is love and love is HE and this is to serve as a small taste and inspiration of what lies beyond for those who truly seek him. HIS is a love without barriers, boundaries or conditions, and thus should each human heart seek to open and give in the same great way as God's. Though this is difficult and requires those to each face great fear of loss or abandonment or solitude, these are only illusions and must be faced and overcome. The true love for another is the one great guide and example that all may relate to send them mightily upon their way.

Of love for the family and children, I will say this: that love among family members is a more complicated thing. There are many factors that do directly affect the roles that each do play and the how's and why's they have arrived in such a place and way. It is not something easily deciphered. For now, it is enough to say that each member of the family is to be treated with love and respect for the other as if all love and Divine Law were present and obeyed. In this manner might all closely related cause and effect between members of the family be quickly resolved and each set on their way to greater glory and knowledge of God. The family as a unit does repeat within itself in different forms and configurations through the ages as ignorance of Divine Law and cause and effect and reincarnation do bind each other to another more and more tightly. To break this cycle and proceed to a place of mutual love and support, each sibling, child, or parent must be treated with love and respect and detached goodwill and never should any action be taken against another in hatred or anger. This is truly the way of the family.

Of love and relations between strangers, I can say this: that each and every man or woman who is met in this life on a more than casual basis does have some significance in the events of your personal history. Their each and every purpose is to resolve some past cause and effect or to give again mutual love and support and detached goodwill. It would behoove the student on the path to greet each with utmost respect and courtesy that all past actions might be undone and the tables cleared forever that you might return home to heaven and not linger here any longer.

DIVINE LAW

The Divine Laws have already been spoken, but let me just say this: that no man shall deprive another of his right to speak freely and of his own mind. It is to each of us the burden of responsibility for our own actions, and the one who does make a habit of showering verbal abuse and lies upon the heads of others shall soon find himself faced with unaccountable and misunderstood misfortune that shall arise from his ill-directed and ill-spoken words. The receiver must learn that anger and pride are futile illusions and want to destroy only himself, and must learn to allow the paltry ill words of others to roll off his back like beads of water on a silent duck.

OF MORALITY

Of morality, it is thus: Morality is the social construction of rules and devices to govern the behavior of the masses and like sheep create in them a common mode of action. The true man of God is guided by a higher principle and has no need for the instructions of the social order to teach him how to act. I was a man who did follow, to the best of my understanding and capabilities, what I did know of Divine Law and this should always be the way.

OF MY MISSION

I did know that it was my mission to serve the Christ when He did come to seek me. When He did gently hold my hand and look into my eyes, I saw the great love and light of a Savior shining back at me, and thus did I know that truly this was my cause and way.

THE GARDEN OF GETHSEMANE

Of the Garden of Gethsemane, I do remember this: Jesus did have us all gathered to hear His final words when a loud knock did come upon the door, and all did stop quickly and fall silent. We did each fear greatly what might transpire next, and the Christ bid us be silent as He went to answer the call. With bated breath, we waited till He did truly return to tell us all was well. Then He brought us closely to say His time was near. He did in turn then give each and everyone of us our sacred initiation into the secrets of His way. He did know then that His days of freedom were ended and that He would be taken soon. He did bid us return on the morrow, and all did leave and go. Then did He turn to John and I, and ask us for our hands, and kneeling down did pray with us to keep the Father's love. Of His words I cannot say, for this must be told by Him.

OF MIRACLES I WITNESSED

Of Jarius' daughter and the bed, there is this: Jarius was a noble soul and had a sickly daughter whom all had left for dead. Jesus did have compassion for the weeping parents and did go to her where she lay, cold and pale, upon her tiny bed. He did rest a hand gently upon her beaded brow and whisper words slowly and softly with a smile of love and light upon His face. After some few minutes, as all were quiet and still, she did begin to stir faintly and slowly come back to life. The parents did joyously laugh and weep and commit themselves to Jesus' following and never left his ways. This I did truly see and remember.

WERE JOHN AND JAMES TWIN BROTHERS?

Of John my one true brother, I can say only this: that we did share the same mother but were not of the same time and day, for truly each had his own time to enter and leave this plane.

THE LAST SUPPER

Of the Last Supper, I can say this: that we were all truly gathered within the house to hear of His last words and eat a final meal. We did take the blood and body of His sustenance, and He did bring us together. We listened as He spoke to us as one and forever were bound together. Now do we return to complete our sacred vows of service and then continue along each our own way.

DRINKING FROM THE CHALICE

When we were gathered at the Supper and the Christ did offer us His Cup, I was the first to reach it and pulled it to my lips. The sweet wine was warm and moistened my parched tongue, and as He slowly spoke the great words of power, I did feel in me a great awakening of knowledge and wisdom and love that I had never known before. It was as if I had swallowed the liquid nectar of the Gods, and a rainbow of love and light had truly settled within my heart.

When I opened my eyes again and let my hand slowly fall, all did stare at me quietly as if I had been in a trance. I do not remember how long or what thoughts did cross my mind—only that I was truly filled with a power and energy of love the likes of which I had never dreamed.

All my brothers did take their turn to drink from the never-ending Cup, and each in turn did look the same with a soft expression of love and gentle wonder upon their shining faces as they did pass the Chalice to the next. As we did then leave to our journeys and pass without the land, each did meet with his eventual demise at the hand of others and fate, but there was no sequential order that linked us to the Cup. We each did only exit and truly leave when our time had truly come.

JESUS' NICKNAME FOR US

Of the "Sons of Thunder" we were truly named by the Christ, for our roaring laughter and jests and the heartiness of our love of life and also, too, because we did tend to noisily set about the streets in search of some brotherly fun with our Roman friends the good soldiers. But this was all in jest and fun, for we did dearly love all. Yet at times, the seriousness of our mission and of the burden of our works did require us to allow some of the great pressure of our love to escape and so we did endure some few minor altercations along the way. This was not meant with ill will or harm for another. But in this time and day, it was as common as a hearty laugh or jest to grapple in this way. Jesus did know and love of our great and roaring hearts and of the passion and zeal with which we did teach and spread His words, and all this put together did lead Him to give us our names.

THE END OF MY MISSION

Before Herod did send me onward, I had in Rome been and spread greatly the word of Christ's teachings to all who would listen there. The fair ladies of that land did especially listen well to my telling of the dangers of congress with those whom they were not in an affair and stately relationship and of the risks this did pose to their health and the growth of their soul. I did share many a great and true secret with those eager maidens, yet eventually this did lead to my death.

Of morals, we have already spoken. And the truth of my words did violate the codes of conduct that had been established there, and so the men grew bitter, and bid Herod end my days. And so to keep his rule of arms, he was compelled to see the sword fall upon my neck.

As I was fearfully awaiting my true and final hour, I did say the sacred prayer the Christ had taught us to commend us to our Maker.

MY BURIAL PLACE

Spain was my true home and final destination, and the great King Alphonso did make me welcome there until my final days. I was sent to him by Gabriel the Angel to protect him and his country for the service they were to render in the Christ's great name, and so I did go and teach them truly of all that Christ had said. They were often beset by invaders and others who wished to do them harm. But as long as they did truly keep to the teachings and the ways of Divine Law and did not become the aggressor or conqueror by force of arms, I did stand by their side and augment their power and protection when I was truly able. Though I did not find my final days upon those beautiful shores, Spain was always in my heart as I did travel and spread of Christ's great message to other lands and places.

I did teach the true word of Christ to Spain and all her peoples after I had been and gone to Northern Africa to help our brothers there. Upon my trip back and to fulfill the request of the Angel Gabriel, I did go to that fair land and from the south begin to travel northward and speak and teach as I did go. My words did truly find warm and loving hearts there, and many orders of monasteries were later created in my wake to keep alive and protected the divine truths that I had shared. So great was their love and devotion to the true teachings that many times I did return to the courts and countryside to share deeper truths and meanings for the many who did gather to hear. Indeed, Spain was the favorite and most successful result of my many travels, and I happily did come to call it home and finally make it my last resting place and mission to serve it always as long as it did keep true to the ways and laws of God.

A MEMORY OF MOTHER MARY

Mary was a patron saint and gifted with many powers, but the ability to materialize the body at a distant location was not one of them. Mary and I did communicate in quieter ways, as we had grown very close and dedicated during my time of training with the Christ, and I had truly promised Him to always watch over her and to always come when I was needed. Thus, when we were once speaking in a quiet way, she did say that she would, as a final act of devotion to her Son, like to always be remembered to those who were dedicated to His ways. And so I did ask the king to build for her a temple in that land I had come to love that Mary might always be remembered by those who loved her Son.

As Patron Saint of Spain

The Spanish did become first in my heart, as I have already told. And when the Moors invaded, I did truly come to their aid. The Moors did desire in their hearts to destroy the monasteries and sacred places that the Spanish had built in Christ's name, and as they did truly uphold and embody the goodness of Divine Law in their ways and hearts, I did rise up with them to truly carry them on. As their patron and protector, it was within my duties and abilities to add to their noble efforts the own force of my love to divert and defeat encroaching enemies who wished to violate the works and teachings of God. And so I did rise up with them against the Moors to stand faithfully by their side and finally send the invaders home.

THE GOSPEL ACCORDING TO JOHN OF ZEBEDEE

OF LOVE

Of love between two people, I can say this: that each man or woman is equally and rightfully entitled to find the love of another. There can be no right force that does keep apart two who truly love one another, for this is to teach them to cherish and respect and listen always to the hidden voice of God speaking through their hearts and to support the other in all endeavors and struggles. When you do join with another in marriage and love, you do accept upon yourself the burden of cause and effect of all their toils and troubles. Though this may seem a good and noble thing, it must be understood fully when contemplating the choice of a partner, for this is truly one of the obligations of marriage and commitment. This is not always a bad thing, for the constant companionship and presence of another is an effective tool for quickly releasing and overcoming large amounts of cause and effect. The Angelic Orders of Cause and Effect will use the partner as a vehicle to present lessons and challenges that are necessary to overcome to progress truly onward on the great path home to God.

Of children and family, this does apply as well, for great are the opportunities within the family circle to make great strides upon the path. Of strangers, a keener eye is required to truly discern the nature of their coming. But if you truly greet and answer all with detached goodwill and respect, then truly shall all your troubles be resolved and quickly shall you progress upon the path back to heaven.

DIVINE LAW

Of Divine Law, this must be said: that the law of God already spoken does truly succeed all others, and this is the rule that must be remembered if one wishes to return home back to heaven.

HOW I WAS CHOSEN?

I did truly know that I was one of the chosen, for when I was walking along the road, an angel did appear before me and quietly sing my name. Then I was told that the Christ did need and await me, and I must go to Him. Thus did I go as I was directed and take my place at His side.

OF JARIUS' DAUGHTER

Of Jarius' daughter, I can say this: that truly was she a sickly child slumped upon the bed. The Christ did enter and bid all leave so He could do His work. Then He called me over to Him to aid Him in His cause. He did use that time to truly show me of the ancient power and art of truly healing and repairing the silver cord to restore life to a cold and listless shell. He did do the sacred prayers and visualizations and did explain to me all that was going on, and then did bid me always remember, lest I not be able to repeat His actions in times of grave danger or need. He did never mention the risks that He did bear nor any terms or conditions under which to use the cure. He only did show me of the way that when we were to be initiated into His number, we would have the skill and power to continue in His way. Of this great story and happening did I truly share with James, though he does tell it much better.

THE GARDEN OF GETHSEMANE

Of the Garden in Gethsemane, we were all truly gathered, the twelve about the One, and He did give to us each and all our sacred initiation into his Circle and way. Then He did bid all others go and return on the morrow for a final gathering together, and to James and I did He return and slowly to the ground did kneel. Upon His knees and with our hands, He looked up to the heavens, and then did speak to His only Father and beg HIM for HIS aid. We did give Him strength as we could and held Him closely as He did go within to commune with the Holy Father until at last He did open His eyes with a peaceful expression on His face and did calmly tell us of all that would occur. And thus when the Disciples did all gather for the final Supper, all did already know of what to expect to hear before He did say a word. This I did truly remember and do tell you.

THE LAST SUPPER

Of the Last great Supper, I can say this: that we were all gathered in a room to hear of His final words and prayer and not a dry eye among us was there, for we were all truly to lose a great friend and teacher. We did all gather round in His final loving embrace, and He bade us be strong and continue on our journeys till we did meet again. Now all is returned and resolved, and we have fulfilled our duties.

THE SANHEDRIN AND NOBLE CITIZENS

Those Jewish nobles and clerics did truly not like the words that I did share for their many and various reasons. Theirs was a philosophy and system that perpetuated the tyranny and superiority of their race and rule and any true message of love and equality did truly threaten all that they had worked so hard to achieve, and so they did threaten me with true bodily injury and harm if I did not desist in my teachings. But this I could truly not do, for I had sworn myself to the service of the Christ, and so did invoke His protection and power to continue in my efforts. And for a time this did dispel their angers and keep me from harm's way. After some time, though, of my continued speaking and teaching, I did sense that their mounting anger would soon breach the lip of my protective veil, and so I did depart to let my teachings settle and search for more fertile lands and hearts.

MY TITLE OF "BELOVED DISCIPLE"

I was the Beloved Disciple of the Christ, for my good temperament and sweet and true devotion to the purity of His works. Though all did love and cherish the Christ, He did feel in me the vulnerability of my sweetness, and the naiveness of my knowing of the world, and this blind and wide-eyed devotion did earn in His heart for me a tender place of love and protection. For truly, the purest of hearts are often the most innocent, too, and little did I know of the world as was the ways and learnings of my faithful brother James who was much more educated and traveled in the ways of the many peoples and cultures and their desires and inhibitions. Thus was I called, and thus did I hold that special place in the Christ's great heart.

THE FOURTH GOSPEL

The Fourth Gospel did come from the pen of James, though I did aid in its creation. We were of a mind and purpose to record truly what we did recall of the Christ's great teachings for all of future generations. And thus did we set out to put our thoughts down that all future seekers of God might have some path and light by which to go along their way. And thus did we record the Fourth Gospel as part of our mission and duty to the Christ.

OF THE TRINITY

Jesus often did speak of His Father and the Word and HE as truly being of one single essence and purpose, yet different manifestations of the same thing. The Word, Truth, Him, man and God, the source of all being were different levels of power, wisdom, and manifestation of the One great Father who does rule us all. Thus was He the earthly incarnation and embodiment of Spirit or truth or the word, which was the true vehicle of the higher inner realms of God or the Father or that all encompassing Universal Intelligence that is known by many names to different peoples and races on this planet and others, for there is truly only One great source of all—One great creator who does bring forth the majesty and splendor of the many imagined universes and worlds of God.

When Jesus did teach of this trinity as the levels of incarnation of God, He did speak in terms of purpose and function of the various subtle parts. Man, Him, was as Its purpose meant to interact in this physical world, and to teach and show how Spirit, the Word, could be received as Truth and made manifest to bring greater light and love into the hearts of those who did seek it. It was a way for man to glimpse of a small flicker of the nature and essence of his creator and purpose, God, who does allow all to exist only because He does love it.

So, all the teachings and techniques and miracles and pains and troubles that the Christ did endure were but to one end to show man of His One true nature and origin and how He could truly return to it. Thus was the Christ's love of humanity so great that He was willing to pay any price to endure any pain or injustice to lead man back to his true home. And thus did He ever seek to purify Himself and make Himself the perfect expression of Spirit, and always be a One who the Word did truly speak to and through to bring its light into the darkest corners of man's closed and sealed hearts.

Thus is it with all saviors and redeemers who do bear great sorrow and pain at the sight and witness of their ignorant brothers and sisters who do cause so much injustice and ill will toward one another as they do live and walk within the blinding veil of illusion that is the way of these treacherous lower worlds. And thus did the Christ, as do all saviors, try to show the way to the light and the return home to all men that He did truly love.

PROPHECY OF REVELATIONS

The visions of Patmos did truly come from another, for I was not the one and do not have the wisdom or remembrance to have placed their contents truly in that great work of truth and noble light that is now known as Revelations.

PATMOS THE SEER: Revelations is a matter of truth given to the hearts of man from the Christ and others to warn of impending disaster. There shall come upon man and earth many things that his mind can scarcely imagine. But this is not yet the time to speak of this great Truth, for it shall truly all be revealed later.

MY FINAL DAYS

I did find my final days in Judea by the shores and did call that fair land my home for many peaceful years. It was a beautiful land with rolling hills of dry beauty that I did enjoy to walk and muse on all that had and did transpire in our wanderings and teachings, for the wisdom the Christ did open in us grew slowly to maturity like a fine wine in a skin. It was a door that was at once opened during the night in the Garden at Gethsemane. But it was a state of power, wisdom, and love that did take time to settle slowly within the heart and unfold gradually over time in each and every soul individually. Judea was the heart of all things for me and truly gave me a safe place to find my quiet repose and allow the great wisdom and truth to seep slowly into my soul.

When I did find that I knew my time was near, I did call upon the Father in the way that the Christ had instructed, and this I did truly say to HIM:

Father, YOU are the ONE and only,
Who I have truly loved and served.

I am YOUR lowly servant,
And have always spread YOUR Word.

Now I do grow weary,
Of long days and nights of work.

And ask YOU to receive me,
That I'll never again know hurt.

These words did I use to softly beseech of HIS great kindness to return me to HIS bosom, and thus was I received at the time of my passing.

THE PASSING OF MOTHER MARY

The lovely Mother Mary was a gentle and true soul who did deeply love her Son and was committed wholly to His works. I and the mother Mary Magdalene were both by her side as she did slip the veil of life and slowly and gently slide softly into her Son and Father's arms on the other side of life. A peaceful countenance and expression did alight upon her face as she did see her Son and Father waiting to greet her with open arms upon the other side of the veil. We were all together in her home down by the sea in the tiny town outside of Judea that was known as Galilee. This was a familiar place to her and one of many fond memories, and so she had chosen to make it the place of her last days with Mary Magdalene always at her side and devoted to her service.

Thus did Mary Magdalene redeem herself of her sins in the service of the Christ, and thus did Mother Mary never lack for any comfort or company in her last years upon this plane. Thus did Mother Mary go to rejoin her Son.

THE FOURTH GOSPEL

The Fourth Gospel was a mutual effort between James and I that was truly completed after his death. Though we did share in its birth and creation together, between our two true hearts, I did provide many ideas and truths and concepts, and James did well commit them to paper. He was the recorder of our thinking and desires and did truly write well over 90 percent of what was said before he left this earth. I did revise and finish our efforts in some small measure after he had left. But the majority of the effort was completed by his true hand, and thus may it be said that the Fourth Gospel truly was written by my noble and glorious brother, yet I did have some small hand in adding some final thoughts.

THE DEAD SEA SCROLLS

James and I were truly approached in dreams by the Angel Gabriel and told to seek of two ancient mystics who lived beyond our lands to record their truths for all to later find and read in what are called the Dead Sea Scrolls. And so we did travel far and wide till we did finally come to that place known as the Valley of Tirmer, and there we did stand before the oracle and listen to its heart. The oracle did tell us truly of all that was to occur with time and the church, and how its books and words would be truly corrupted by those seeking power and wealth, and how 2,000 years later there would come a need to bring back great light into the fallen teachings. There was another sage, and he was also hidden from view. Thus were there two oracles consulted, one at Tirmer, and the other at Adelphi and each did give of their hearts. And so did we combine their ancient wisdom and visions and truly record their words for all to hear and remember.

And so we were told and did truly record the great truths of the true meaning of the Second Covenant and Book of Revelations so that they would be found and brought to light upon those later days when they would be truly needed. And thus did the oracle bless the Scrolls and imbue in them the life and consciousness all their own that they might have their own power to remain preserved and protected and to call to their seekers when those true souls did return to find them in their hiding place. Thus did we return to our land and hide the Scrolls where they were found as instructed by the angel, and thus do they remain today, waiting for their great truth and light to be fully exposed to right the badly sailing and mistaken church from its far off course of passage. Thus were the Scrolls committed and delivered by myself and James.

THE GOSPEL
ACCORDING TO
PHILIP

OF LOVE

Of love with another, I can say only this: that man and woman are put together such that they might become as one. One of heart, one of mind, one in unity, one of purpose. This is truly the example of how each Soul must come to love God and join with HIM and enter into HIS shared purpose, for it is not a marriage of harmony or truth if the two thus joined should serve at opposite ends. Though there may be difficulties and trials, these must be kept in proper perspective and the greater good always in mind. Thus might all great seekers find themselves eventually home with God.

Of love within the family, this can also be said: that each family group does come together to learn to find a single purpose that does bind them as a whole. When souls do come as a group to move back to God, it is with an air of mutual love and support for all the great difficulties of their true and noble endeavors. If there is love and support from others who do truly love each other and understand the higher purpose each does serve and the nature of the difficulties and challenges to be encountered along the way, then the trials are made less burdensome if he knows that his family is always near for encouragement and support. This is not to say that the parents should take on or carry the child's burdens for him, for each must learn his own true lessons and pay and receive in the true coin, yet there can be the element of love, support, and guidance to aid each on the path.

Of love between strangers, I can say this: that each man or woman whom one does encounter can be seen as a face of himself and must be loved and accepted and cherished with compassion and understanding as one should also be of his own faults and foibles. Thus will the man of God move quickly on the path back to heaven and be at the Father's side.

OF MORALITY

Of morality, I can say this: that there is not a single code that may govern the actions of man truly, save for the Divine Laws of God. Of these, Jesus has already spoken. Yet let me only say this: that morality is a social convention, and Divine Law is a rule of God, immutable and inviolable without the greatest of repercussions of the Law of Cause and Effect. Thus, each must thoroughly learn and understand and obey the Divine Laws of God that they might proceed with haste upon the path back to God.

HOW I WAS CHOSEN?

I did truly know that I was of the chosen when I did see high in the night a bright star that brought me to the Christ. When I did tell Him of my story, He said, "It was I that did call you thus to add you to my number, for truly do I need you here." Thus did I remain at His side and humbly serve His mission—even to this day.

THE LAST SUPPER

Of the Last Supper, it was a sad and tearful affair. We were all great with sorrow that the One we loved should be taken from us and sent on to other realms. He did promise us to return and bade us be

strong and continue with our works. Then He gave us all His blessing and love and with a heavy heart did turn and go.

THE FEEDING OF THE FIVE THOUSAND

Jesus had truly spoken at the Sea at Galilee, and after he Had finished, the hungry poor people did seek to fill their stomachs now that
their hearts were full. Jesus did softly speak to the Disciples and give
them some secret words to have each utter, as if they were an extension of the Christ's own body and arms, and so out of their baskets
and pitchers did flow a seemingly endless supply of bread and wine.
The Christ truly had used the Disciples as His vehicles to share of the
great love within His heart for all peoples, and so bring them to His
bosom and bind them eternally to His word. For as they did eat of
His flesh and drink of His blood, this was a sacred initiation and was
the true purpose and intent though He did share this with none.

Jesus did have many and varied techniques and ways to bind His
followers to His heart, and many of His miracles and deeds were truly
done, not because the soul in question was deserving or needy, but
because the Christ did know that it would take many lifetimes for each
soul to truly achieve perfection. And so He did desire to have each soul
bound tightly to His ways that they might always seek the truth and
love in earnest and so progress rapidly onward to heaven. He did not
well foresee the error of His thinking or that His techniques would
be so perverted and so did incur much unnecessary burdens from those
whom He had bound too closely to Himself who now had no access
to the true teachings and so did many wrong deeds in His name. And
so were the 5,000 thus fed and bound tightly to Him.

THE RESURRECTION

Jesus did return for His brief stay again in the body when it was lying as a useless shell in the cave. He did truly reenter it and raise it from the dead to a walking, real man of flesh and blood and feelings. He did know that He did have to fulfill several important objectives. First, to give the Disciples proof of His true nature and of the cause and ways of His teachings. Second, to withdraw His body from the Romans that they might repent of their evil ways and also not desecrate His form or allow it to be misused for wrong purposes. And third, to say farewell to his Mother and to Mary Magdalene whom He did truly love. Thus did He return again and walk among us before taking His physical form off to other realms.

MY TRAVELS

I did travel softly and spread the teachings of the Christ in a quiet and unassuming manner, for I did see how my Brothers did quickly fall and desired not to join their number. I did feel that I could better serve the Christ by moving quietly and gently and serving those souls who I did encounter along the way. And so I did travel west to Spain and France and England, and farther upon the Northern shores to Finland and Denmark and Norway and Sweden, and finally did return to the East and warmer climes in what is now Turkey and Iran. I wandered quietly and slowly and never did stay long in any one place but always did seem to find those one or two people who truly did need of my gentle ways, and thus did I serve of the Christ and His works.

I did spend some many years in Caesarea as I did toil upon my travels but did not call this my home. This was merely a place where I did have good and trusted friends who did look after me and was centrally located for my constant travels to other places. Thus did it seem that this was a place of contentment and quiet living, but this was not the case, for it was merely a place to safely return to when I did grow tired of always moving about.

THE GOSPEL ACCORDING TO BARTHOLOMEW

OF LOVE

Of love between two partners, I can say this: that love is a gift from God that does truly separate man from all other forms of life. Though some animals do find a sort of attraction and bond for one another, this is not the same. Man is given love as a gift from God to begin him on his great journey home. It is the first true step toward that endless journey back to the Father's side. Love is a taste of the nectar that does bloom eternally within the heart once it is opened and able to receive and give of this fountain of all great life.

Man must learn how to overcome fear and truly love one another in the family, as a partner, and as a stranger, for this is truly the key to all things. Love to some is just a word, but it is indeed a frequency to be truly understood and mastered and is the key to all the higher worlds. It is not to be confused with the silly human emotion that is driven by hormones or desire to act out some fantasy or misplaced devotion. It is something of a higher order that truly does not even require the union of the flesh to be experienced. It is a simple good-willed nature and caring for others that does alight a great fire within the breast and force upon the face a gentle open smile that has no need or basis for return. It is a simple gift of giving and may be sent freely and truly to all who do seek and desire of it, and it is truly the first and most important step back to heaven. Of love between man and woman or any other, or between children or strangers this is all the same, for souls are souls and each deserving and desiring of all the great love of God and of each other.

MORALITY

Of morality, I can say this: that this is a strange notion created by false prophets and leaders to keep power and control over the unconscious masses. If each man were to know and understand Divine Law, then morality would not be a word that did even exist. For now, it is used by those seeking power and control and for social reasons to falsely elevate one above another. There may be no true judge of a man's actions or ways except by the Divine Law spoken by the Christ.

HOW I WAS CHOSEN?

I did truly know that I was to be His servant when He did come to me upon the road and ask me of my dreams. Before I could reply, He did proceed to tell me all that was buried deep within my heart. Thus did I know that I was truly to follow and serve Him all my days.

THE LAST SUPPER

Of the Last Supper, this must be said: that it was a somber and sobering affair. We all did know that we were to lose our friend and teacher—and even our own lives. Yet none was bitter or angry at the Roman ignorance—only deeply saddened and with compassion for the misfortune soon to come upon man. All we ever did want was to return souls home to God, yet this was misunderstood and greatly feared. And we did pay the price.

MY FINAL DAYS

I did die in those cold and forbidding mountains of Armenia as I was fleeing there to escape the persecution of soldiers of the king of that land. I had been teaching to his peoples of the fair Christ's true wisdom and love, and he did become afraid of the freedoms the people did begin to seek and desire. So I fled in the company of some followers to escape his soldiers and sought refuge in the cold forbidding peaks of those mountains of that land. We did journey high into the craggy peaks and precipices, seeking to elude capture, but alas we did not succeed and so were taken by the soldiers to be returned to the city and the king.

However, this was not to be the case, for as we did begin our journey back to his fair palace and lands, we did encounter some difficulty and were truly killed in an encounter with those independent and strong willed mountain people who did detest his rule. And thus were we as prisoners of the soldiers killed along with all the rest, and thus did I end my days upon earth as an unfortunate consequence of senseless violence against the rulers of that land.

When we were truly taken by the king's men and I was a captive with the others, I did know that I truly was to die, and so I did commend myself to the Maker on the night of our arrest. I did speak of my heart frankly and with great fear, and this is what I did say:

Father, I do fear that the end of my mortal days have come,
And I seek solace in YOUR arms, as I do return to YOUR home.

I have traveled far and wide to give of YOUR true teachings,
And now I do fear for my transition into heavenly reaches.

Thus did I beseech of HIS protection, and thus was it granted as I did fall before the mountain bandits and did feel neither pain nor agony as they did commit terrible horrors to my body. And thus do the people there revere me for the innocence of my slaughter and the love I did always bestow upon their hearts.

Of Miracles I Performed

Of miracles, there is much to say. But this will I truly tell: Of the many deeds and services that I did perform in the Christ's great name, there could be created a great and long list. But for now I will answer your queries.

The daughter of King Polymius was a child of fair and simple ways and did truly bear the mark of madness upon her face, and so was I called forth to see what I could do. I did peer softly within her heart and did see the misalignment of the subtle bodies that was creating an improper connection between the sheaths of the mental and causal plane and so did know that true and proper instructions were not making it clearly for expression in the lower body. This condition did truly manifest itself as lunacy or madness.

I did promise the king to do my best and so did quietly begin to speak the healing incantation that the Christ had given to us. As I did do the technique and bring the love within me and focused its light upon the error, I did begin to see in my mind's eye the realignment and healing of the tear. And thus when I had completed and the fine fabric of her mind was repaired, she did truly open her eyes softly and for the first time begin to speak in calm tones and complete sentences. And thus was she truly healed and the king was won to our side.

The exorcism of evils was a common thing to do at that time, for there were many negative spirits that did seek expression in man and he had not yet sufficiently developed his inner defenses to keep most

things at bay. Thus, on many occasions was I asked to, and I did perform, simple exorcisms to rid the victim of his infection and give him
the light of the Christ's protection to shield him from further harm.

The technique was oft repeated and similar in each and every case
and did occur in the manner thusly. First, the subject was taken to a
quiet and private place and the family was asked to leave. Then I alone,
or with another, would go into quiet contemplation and begin to see
their face. As they did begin to form and be seen in my mind's eye,
the healing light of Christ would be placed within and about them
to drive the darkness away. This light was then energized and
activated by repeating the sacred words that the Christ had given to
us. After the appointed time, the body would begin to hold and
embody the light of its own accord and be safely healed and returned
to its former state. Then the victim was given one of the Christ's prayers
to protect him from further harm.

Those wishing of Christ's same protection today can daily repeat
the "Prayer for the Living" and this shall truly keep him out of reach
of the arms of negative entities that do wish to join with him.

OF ANGELIC INTERVENTION

Of the angels and their interventions, I can say this: that often did
I come across those who did seek some boon from the Christ on
behalf of their need or that of another, and sometimes I did see these
matters resolved before I was able to take any true action by the inter-
vention of their angel. Typically, the process did occur thusly: I would
hear of a man or woman's request and sense a gentle presence and would
inwardly ask that in the name of the Christ, if any protective or angelic
being were present, for them to truly do all they could to aid the situation, and I did offer my energy and strength as additional power and
connection to the love of God and the Christ to aid in the resolution.

Thus would I bid the seeker return on the morrow or in a week's time to allow the angel the opportunity to do their duty. And on many occasions, the seeker would return with joyous light in their eyes to gladly tell me that their prayers had been answered and all their needs resolved, and thus did I know that the angels were truly present and at work.

THE ARMENIAN CHURCH

The Armenian Church has truly loved me for lo these many years, because when they did finally learn that I did perish at their own hands and did also remember of my great love and teachings, then they did hold me in their memories to honor of my deeds. And so were the teachings of the Christ and of my simple words always remembered and revered.

THE GOSPEL
ACCORDING TO
MATTHEW

OF LOVE

Of love, I can say this: that many are the days and nights that each does pine for the true love of another. But truly this is not the way, for none shall find the great and true love they do seek from another's heart before they have found and known of the true love of God. Though a brief moment in the sun in the glow of another's love and its sweet embrace may give the inspiration for the great journey onward, this is only a small taste to set you on your way and must not be mistaken for the final goal.

The love of God does fill a heart completely and dissolve all fear and anxiety that the one with a heart full of the love of God might love all of humanity with no fear of rejection or loss. This is truly the ideal and a state to be aspired to, but it is a journey and a process and one is not to get frustrated with his progress along the way if it is not as rapid as he would desire, for there are truly many compounding factors. The love of God is freely given to all and may be found and truly received in a single lifetime. Yet it takes a level of devotion, care, and discipline that most are not capable of achieving. For many, the job in this life is simply to learn to love a little better and take that next small step of progress toward the goal. However, once the nectar of God's love is truly tasted, then there is no force in all the worlds that can hold man back from his desire to know and be one with the infinite love of God.

Love, whether it is in the family, with strangers, or with another who you do hold dear is a single and unique purpose for each. For some, to show a glimpse of what the love of God can be, for others it is a final state of completion and enjoyment after the long journey toward self-perfection. It is to each and his own to discern what to him love is and must be to aid him on his journey. It will change with time and experience, and this is good and well. However, this must always be remembered: that love is a piece of the grace of God and not something to be taken lightly. Do not mock or scorn or take in jest the true love given to or received from another, for this is to mock the sacred nature of God itself. This is a sacred gift and feeling and is to be held with the greatest reverence and respect.

OF MORALITY AND DIVINE LAW

Of morality and Divine Law, I can say this: that morals are truly the laws of behavior for the weak and feeble-minded who are not able to make intelligent and proper choices for themselves. The true guide to all actions and behavior is simple and may be found in the Divine Laws that the Christ has already spoken.

HOW I WAS CHOSEN?

Of my work and mission for the Christ, I can say this: that I was truly knowing of my purpose and mission to be at His side when I did receive a knock at my door one day and find Him and Peter standing there to greet me. I did ask them in to sit, and Peter spoke their minds. He did ask me truly what I did seek in life, and truly I did answer from my heart: to only serve God in all HIS ways and actions. Then the Christ did rise and place His hand upon my shoulder, and I did see the white light about Him and feel of His great love. Thus did I know that I had found the Master and was truly to serve Him for the rest of my days.

How I Received My Nickname

The noble name of "Levi" was gratefully bestowed on me by the Christ for my unerring and total devotion to His ways and to His cause. On many occasions did I forsake all other obligations and duties of all other callings and places to be by His true side. And so did my unflinching devotion and belief in His cause and ways give Him and all others great comfort and sustenance, and so was I awarded the nickname "Gift of God."

The Sermon on the Mount

The Sermon on the Mount was an inspiration and great and uplifting prayer and was never forgotten or not remembered by any that did truly hear of its true heart. Jesus did ascend the Mount that He should address the gathered crowd and did seek and desire to be placed such that His voice should well carry to all the assembled throngs. He did wish to speak of His teachings and Gospel of love in its many varied forms and faces, and so did He gather all around to hear what He would say.

And as He spoke, there did come to be seen a great and fiery image that did hang about His head. And as the words did flow from His heart with truth and love and compassion, the bright white light of love did engulf Him and all the people did stare in disbelief and fear as the light of the love of God did truly manifest before them. And thus did Jesus' heart and teachings and words begin to flow directly and without any sound into the hearts of all who were present.

When it was over and done and began to gently fade, the image of Jesus standing on the Mount did return and all did quietly shake their heads in wonder, for none could well remember what had truly transpired. They had been taken on a sacred journey. Yet when they did return to their normal and everyday state of awareness, they were unable to recall what they had truly seen and experienced of higher realms.

And thus is the Sermon on the Mount well-loved and remembered by all, but few are there who truly do know and understand what actually did transpire.

CHRIST CAME TO SERVE

The Son of Man came not to be served but to serve,
and to give His life as a ransom for many.

The phrase on Jesus' service has a clear and simple meaning: The Christ was a great Savior and of highly developed standing, and there was no thing that any on earth could truly give Him that He did desire, for He did have the Father's love and protection. And what greater achievement or pleasure could man seek on earth? Thus all that did remain for the Christ was to give of all that He did know and had learned to others, and thus honor and serve the One who did hold Him dear. And thus did the Christ come to Earth truly to only serve others, but not to be served Himself.

Of the ransom of His life, there is this: Jesus did come to truly offer the great love that He did have within His heart for all of man; however, He did in this process and in His ignorance take on the cause and effect and debts of many He did heal and give succor to. Thus, when He was called to make payment in the true coin, He did offer up Himself in place of all who He had aided and thus was His death the ransom paid to save all souls who He did truly love and serve.

BEING TAX COLLECTORS

James and I did select the position and occupation as tax collectors for a specific and deliberate reason: It did allow us to make constant and repeated contact with all the citizens of the lands without raising fear or suspicion or alarm, and also because the people would truly listen to what we did have to say when we did come, for who was there that did wish to risk offending the tax collector of the king. And so were we able to quietly visit and speak with many people and spread the truth of God.

THE GATHERING AT CAPERNAUM

The Christ did appear at a gathering at Capernaum to share of His great heart, and I was among the crowd that did gather to hear what He would say. And so as He did begin to speak, I did start to see about His head a halo of golden light. I turned to James and asked him truly if he did see it there and he did agree, but no others did seem to have the same vision that we did. And thus did we later follow and speak to the Christ and ask Him of our vision. And He did reply that our sight was a gift from God to be put in the service of His ways and works, and He would be honored to have us by His side. And so did we begin to follow Him, and I did eventually, through my great love and devotion, earn the title "Levi."

THE STORM UPON THE SEA

We were truly out on the sea with the Christ when a small and intense storm did begin to blow about us. We did fear that all would be lost, but Jesus remained unafraid. He stood calmly at the bow and asked why we did lack such faith in the providence and protection of the Lord, and we all did not have any suitable answer. So He then did bid us enter into quiet contemplation and repeat the holy words. And as we did fall quiet and began to do as He said, the raging storm abated and all became quiet instead.

When we had all finished and returned to normal states, one did cry out in question to ask if He did care if we lived or perished. The Christ replied that all would always commence as God had truly planned for us. And if we did keep our faith in Him and our wits about, then all would always proceed according to how it was to unfold, for it was not a matter if He did care for our lives or not, for what was to truly transpire had been written in the stars, and it was His only concern and duty to give to us the knowledge and wisdom and power to fulfill the missions that we had agreed to assume.

And so He did want to teach us that when troubles and fear did face us, but it was not yet our time to go to truly keep our wits about us and use the tools and techniques we had been given to keep our ships afloat and on the proper course. Thus was our experience with the storm upon the Sea.

No Miracles in Nazareth

Nazareth was the true home and birthplace of the Christ, and He did often return there to visit of His friends and family and other peoples but never did perform any miracles. Jesus did know that if He did make a practice of doing those things there that that town would become known as a sacred place of pilgrimage and worship, and the attention and fame and glory that would surround such things would attract undesirable attention and so put in danger and harm's great way those whom He did truly love. Thus was He always careful never to do any miracles or healings in and around the town.

THE LAST SUPPER

Of the Last Supper, this may truly be said: that we were all solemnly gathered for our final meal with the Christ. We knew we were to lose a dear friend and Brother. Yet none had tears to cry, for we all did realize that His going was only a temporary thing and that we would all be together again upon the other side. Thus did we break bread and drink together and give Him our final love and admiration.

MY FINAL DAYS

I did truly die at the hands of the Sanhedrin in Ethiopia where they had sent me there. The long arm of the Jewish clerics did reach even to that far land, and they did greatly fear of my return and teachings and so did dispatch secret soldiers to find me and prevent my return. And so as I did teach and share the truths of Christ in that dark and faraway land, the soldiers did come upon me in the night and quietly take my life. I did not know of their coming and so was unprepared and did not adequately prepare myself for my passing, but this I did manage to pray:

> *Father, I have done YOUR work,*
> *And now do return.*
>
> *Take me softly to YOUR breast,*
> *For I do fear this passage.*

And thus did I die quickly and was received to the Father's arms on that dark and hot night faraway in Ethiopia.

THE GOSPEL ACCORDING TO JAMES
(BROTHER OF MATTHEW)

OF LOVE

Of love, there is only this to say: that all the great and noble and beautiful and true actions that have ever been created or taken to truly inspire man have been born of the heart of love. Of love between partners, much has already been said, and of children, and strangers, too, but there also is this: Love is a seemingly mysterious thing until it is truly experienced, and then it becomes all one can think or talk about, and the fixation of all one's true efforts.

Once the heart does begin to open and allow the love and light of God to enter, then does the man or woman begin to finally feel the true nature of Soul and its existence in the higher realms. This love is a divine gift from God that is what enables and drives all of the functions and objects and experiences of all the worlds of creation. Soul and man and all that is seen and known and experienced exists because God loves it. There is nothing more. So love must always be held and considered a sacred thing and never abused or mistreated. The heart of another is a gentle and invaluable gift and is to be always treated with care.

MORALITY AND DIVINE LAW

Of morality and Divine Law, there is this: that morality is nothing more than a puff of hot air to gain control and power over others. It is a fabrication of the social consciousness and nothing more. Divine Law does truly give the rules by which man must judge his behavior, and all else is nothing to be seriously considered or weighed in the process.

How Was I Chosen?

I did truly know that I was to be one of the Christ's chosen when I did see alight upon the branch a dove with a piece of cloth in its beak. It did drop this cloth to me and fluttered about impatiently until I did rise and follow. I was led to the great Christ's side and there did I see the place where His robe had torn. He received the piece I had with a gentle and loving smile and bid me to join His Circle and thus did I never leave His side.

How I Received My Nickname

I was truly known as "James the Less" for many varied reasons. My brother and I did have the gift of sight bestowed on us by God, but it was a thing and talent that he truly was the stronger, but this is not why I was called thus.

Upon our many travels and in our duties as tax collectors, we were oft called upon to carry out some activities and requests that others considered unpleasant, addressing those of questionable repute or nature, traveling to unsafe places, carrying the Word to areas of danger or where we had been forbidden. And it often did fall upon my shoulders the brunt of these unpleasant deeds, and thus did I earn the nickname of James the Lesser, for my willingness to always do what did need to be done, no matter what the circumstance, and to do it in such a way and manner as to return safely and secretly to continue always with our works.

It was a subtle play on words that the Christ did smile as He did say my name, for He did consider my deeds great and true in nature but did also know of my shy nature and dislike of oratory and the bestowments of fame. And so to honor my quiet nature and desire to remain unknown, He did bestow on me the gentle compliment of James the Less, as all who did truly know of me and my ways would understand the purpose and the meaning and honor of my desires and wishes.

THE LAST SUPPER

Of the final Supper, I can say this: that it was a somber evening and all were heavy of heart at the Christ's soon leaving for other realms. Though we did all understand and were sad to see Him go, we were chastened by His words to remain strong and continue with our works. And so we gently wiped the corner of our eyes and did gather close for His final embrace and prayer, and then He did leave us to our own thoughts and quietly slipped out the door.

MY FINAL DAYS

I did bear a long and productive life until my final days at the hands of the Sanhedrin. I had traveled with my brother to the far off lands by the sea, and there we did gather a crowd to hear of our words as was our custom and manner. We did speak to them gently and truly as was our custom and manner.

As we had truly begun to finish, the Roman soldiers did roughly enter the crowd and order all to return to their homes and leave. Matthew and I did quietly leave to our own ways. But as I was walking quietly, one did catch my arm and roughly pull me aside. I did not wish to betray my brother. And as we had agreed that our duties and missions were more important than each other, he did continue on his way as I was taken by the soldiers. They did take me to stand and answer for my actions, and I was condemned to death by the axe and the beheading. Thus did I spend my final night in a Roman prison beseeching for the grace of the Father. I did commend myself to HIM truly, and this is what I did say:

> *Father, the law does judge me truly,*
> *For what I have said and done in YOUR name.*
>
> *I do ask that YOU receive me,*
> *As one who has carried YOUR ways.*
>
> *The way is long and hardened,*
> *And always have I carried YOUR heart.*
>
> *To give to all willing seekers,*
> *Who did wish to know its secrets.*

Thus did I beseech of the Father's protection and when the sword did fall upon my neck was quickly and painlessly taken from the body and returned to the great Christ's side.

My Ministerial Travels

Matthew and I did travel a fair amount, though our duties as tax collectors and our ministry to those souls we did teach that way did occupy much of our time. However, we did go to the lands of Judea, Cairo, Turkey, Iran, Iraq, Northern Africa, Spain, and Morocco in support of our other Brothers and to carry on the Christ's great work.

We spoke of many topics as we did gather those around us, but foremost for our times was how to live a true and loving life in the ways of God, how to know and do HIS will, and how to respect the community and laws you lived in and also find your way back to God within the boundaries that you did share with your community and others. We did see the paths of our many Brothers as they ended poorly upon the cross and in other ways, and we did feel that we could best serve our Master to teach of ways that the spiritual truths and goals could be achieved, yet with one still keeping his head. And so we eschewed miracles and public healings and instead traveled little and worked quietly to spread the Gospel to open hearts and willing ears and thus to continue in the ways of Christ.

MY MESSAGE
TO TODAY'S FLOCK

For those of the flock today, I would teach this: that although I have been gone for many thousand years and more, these are some things of importance that do remain the same. The most powerful means of instruction is by example and living, walking proof of the truths and principles that one of Christ and God do hold dear. And thus would the focus of my efforts and ministry be to be at large in a productive role within my community that did put me in contact in a regular way with the people that did need me, and by my example and gentle ways lead others to the truths that it was my mission to share. In this way can all be accomplished without being forceful or pushy, as does violate Divine Law and the ways of God but does also show truly of the example of love and light and how it may save a man. Thus should I conduct myself and my affairs to truly serve the will of God.

THE GOSPEL ACCORDING TO SIMON THE ZEALOT

OF LOVE

Truly did I see of love with different eyes from all others, for there was no man, woman, or child who could truly steal my heart from God. All my days and nights and journeys were spent with the great and unquenched desire upon my heart to know more of the nature and extent of his infinite good. I was truly possessed of this desire, and so did not have much experience with any other.

Of love though, I can say this: that it is an all-consuming fire once it is lit truly within the breast of man, and once he does feel of the sweetness of God's gentle breath upon his heart and ear, then there is no other thing in this universe that can tempt him to any other goal. It is all there remains for him to only ascend to greater heights of glory, wisdom, and power, and aid those others truly on their own path home.

MORALITY AND DIVINE LAW

Of morality and Divine Law, there can be said this: that if one has the latter, he needs not of the former, for the Divine Laws do give one the proper means for making all decisions. And when anyone is in doubt of what is the true and proper action, he must only go within his heart and in true and quiet reflection can gently say the name of Christ, and all answers will be to him given.

My Political Affections

The Zealots were a group of followers of a radical tradition and desired of change in the ways that the Romans did rule our lands. However, this does not pertain to my nickname although I was a member and supporter of their efforts. I was truly given the name of "Zealot" by the Christ for the fervor of my belief in the truth and ways of his teachings, and by my all-consuming desire to always know and learn more of the ways of God. And thus was neither my head nor affections swayed by any earthly pleasures, and I did remain wholly and singularly focused and committed to the work and mission of the Christ.

Travel and of Miracles

Miracles and healings were a common service to be performed for the poor and oppressed peoples, and I did perform many of both in Christ's name. I was skilled and passionate as a worker of His wonders, and I did show little restraint when the opportunity to do some good did arise. Indeed, this did mightily contribute to my final days, as the Sanhedrin did not appreciate of the prophets and servants of Christ to be demonstrating powers that did surpass their own. And thus did I perform exorcisms, heal madness, protect innocents from harm, lift blindness, dissolve infirmity, and return lepers to a whole and healthy state of being. There were so many difficulties that man did face each day that finding opportunities to utilize the sacred gifts never was a difficulty.

I did go to Persia with the others to spread the good word there, but we were met with a forceful resistance who truly did not wish to hear our words. Still did we continue with our works and move onward spreading of the Christ's message to those closed and forbidden lands. Persia was a land of kings who truly did fear of losing their power, and so were we watched closely to see that we did not encourage rebellion or acts against the throne. But we did preach our simple message of love and truth, and so although many were suspicious, we did come to no harm.

How I Was Chosen?

I did know that I truly was to serve at His side when He did give to me a scroll that bore the great words of truth that I did seek. When I did read of those few words, I did know that He was the true Son of God and I was to stand at His side forever. The words on the scroll were this: "Let no man or woman or any other put any truth or law or action above those that God does give to HIS sons and daughters to guide them on their path home." Thus did I know that He did speak truth and I truly was to follow.

The Last Supper

Of the Last Supper, there is this to say: that we were all gathered and quiet and saddened that the day had come to say goodbye and so much remained left undone. We did know that we would all have to journey long and far without Him until we would find ourselves at this place again to finally resolve all matters. We did bid Him farewell and silently return to our own thoughts, yet each kept his own counsel. It is only now that we all do come together again to finish what we started.

My Final Days

We were deep within Persia doing our work there when we did come upon a group of villagers who did fear of our presence and words. We did seek to calm them. But this was not to be done, and they did set upon us with stones and curses and hate. We did flee back to Jerusalem although we narrowly did escape their clutches. As the Sanhedrin did wish to put our heads on the ground and sever them from our bodies, we did allow the rumors of our death in Persia to circulate and grow, for this did create for us a temporary protection. I did then go to Egypt to commence with labors there, but this was not to be my destination, for as I was disguised and did travel unbeknownst with a group of strangers, we were set upon by bandits along a dark and isolated stretch of road. And thus were all dispatched to the Father, and I among their number. Thus did the rumors of my death in Persia grow into fact and legend, but indeed they were not true.

As I did await my final execution in the flurry of activity and fear, I did commend myself to the Father, and this is what I did say:

> *Father, the end does set upon me,*
> *In wicked and violent ways.*
>
> *I have given of all I had within me,*
> *To speak and spread YOUR words.*
>
> *Now as they do seek me,*
> *I come to YOU with haste.*
>
> *And ask YOU to receive me,*
> *That I might finally join YOU at last.*

Thus did I commend myself to the Father and thus did I suffer little and was well received when I did enter upon the other side.

THE GOSPEL ACCORDING TO JUDAS, SON OF JAMES

OF MY NICKNAME

"Thaddeus" was the name given me by the Christ for my noble deeds and service. In those ancient days and tongues, it truly did mean "One who served well and wisely," for a "Thad" was one of the ancient forgotten lands that were known for their hard labor and toils and unerring devotion to a cause and purpose. Jesus did tell us of the parables and stories of His memories of this land. And so it did become known among us and so because He did recognize and truly appreciate the disciplined and absolute commitment of my labors did He hence call me "The Thaddeus," for how I did remind Him of those whose memories He did hold dear in His heart from that strange and far off land.

THE SANHEDRIN AND ROMAN OCCUPATION

At the time of Jesus' rising and ascension of His powers and popularity and teachings, there was a plague of man upon the lands of Israel, and it was the Roman rule. Those foul soldiers and their clerics did indeed malign and destroy and contaminate all that they did touch and so wreak a holy havoc upon our beautiful and sacred lands. The clerics did endure their presence, for it did support and extend their ill-begotten power, but this was truly not a noble service of them to their own peoples or lands.

There were within the numbers of us many hidden factions who did seek to return Israel to its rightful owners by one means or another. Some did advocate violence, others different means. But all did share the common goal of seeing our lands return and led by one of its native sons who did share a true love and understanding of its peoples and its soil and did not merely view it as a tax generating colony amidst the many other spoils of war and conquest.

And so, as the Christ did begin to grow in renown and popularity, it was put forth that He should begin preparations to take back by force what had been taken from us wrongly, and the several and disparate factions did agree to unite behind the Christ if He would lead the way.

I did support His movement in this direction, for I did truly know that His would be a rule that was just and true and based on the Divine Laws of God and not the corrupt laws of man. And thus did I suggest to Him that to ensure His backing and support of the others and to show the Romans and clerics of the breadth and depth of His true nature and power and of the love the Father did bear Him that He should give some discernible and direct demonstration of His powers and thus begin all actions. The Christ, though He was deeply moved by our confidence in His efforts, did decline, for His was an effort and campaign that never could be won by force, but only by love. For this was the rule of Divine Law in these matters, and thus did He decline to lead our number but continued instead with the works and efforts of His ministry.

The Roman infection was a curse upon our lands that did rob us of our dignity, freedoms, and many other liberties and did always serve to remind of our fair peoples that they did serve the whims of another by rule of force and not by law of love. And so did the resentment and anger simmer and boil in all who did long to see our government return to those who would create and administer it out of a love for its soil and peoples and not for the wealth it could bring to far off treasuries.

The Maccabees were one of several factions that did seek to return to power a group or leader who would truly be a servant of the people. And although they did endorse certain extreme tactics and philosophies of operation and conduct, I did support the intention of their efforts to secure for Israel a place and station of independence that would truly allow her to dictate her own ways and decisions and thus did I lend them my heart and hands whenever I was able and it did not interfere with my duties for the Christ or His teachings of Divine Law and comportment of one's own behaviors.

MY EXPERIENCE WITH KING ABGAR

The King Abgar of Edessa was truly possessed by madness and I was called forth to see what could be done. He had an affliction that did render him incapable of speaking or seeing clearly, and his words and eyes did go in random and haphazard directions. And so was he kept from view and his regents did rule in his stead as various cures and treatments were sought to relieve of his condition. He had truly been bitten in the night by some animal with infection, and now this did spread into his heart and gradually direct his deterioration into his own true madness.

I did immediately detect the pollutants circulating in his blood and so did begin my proceedings. We did retire to a private chamber, and I did bid him sit quietly as he was able, and he was restrained in my view and near me. Then did all leave and I did enter into quiet contemplation to truly commence with my labors. Once I had gone within, I could truly see the madness circulating as dark spots of disease and illness circulating within his blood and the many tiny layers and currents of life within the subtle bodies. I did begin the procedure to bring him into the light, and so let the love and power of God cleanse him of all impurities. And so, after a period, his light again began to shine and the impurities within his systems were gone and he did now bear the mark of health and the loving light of Christ.

I did return to normal wakefulness and did untie his bonds and gave him a holy and powerful prayer of Christ to sustain his protection and keep him from future harm. And thus did we walk side-by-side from the room, and Edessa was returned to its king. As this did create for our number a powerful friend and ally, I was given the protection and services of his ranks, and so did travel his lands spreading the Christ's message and helping all that I did encounter as I passed within all that he did truly rule and govern. And thus did the people of Edessa receive and joyously learn of the sacred teachings of Christ.

Spiritual Travels and Final Days

The twelve provinces of the Persian Empire was a region beset by ignorance and strife and seeking of a solution and truth to guide them away from their fears and angers and apprehensions. I did travel there with others to bring the light of Christ to their eyes and hearts, yet it was a difficult task. Often, the light of truth and love does truly well frighten those who are accustomed to the dark, and its piercing rays can burn those tender eyes and hearts unless great care is taken to gradually open and adjust their vision. I was a patient and loving teacher and did truly understand the time that would be required to open of their hearts and show them of an alternative way of being.

However, Simon was less patient in his zealous love of God and his full confidence and knowing of the power of its healing. And thus did he open the full of his love and power upon a gathered crowd, and the intensity of the brilliance and light of his love and wisdom did singe their gentle hearts and so they did flee in confusion and fear, for they could not understand or fathom what they had truly beheld; it simply was too much for their lowly state of awareness.

I did warn Simon to truly curb his passion and enthusiasm lest our efforts did bring us to some poor end because of the fear it did engender in those who were not ready to yet embrace the light. But my admonishments fell upon deaf ears, and Simon did continue in the confidence of his own ways. Thus did we come upon a crowd that was gathering and did see us. And before we could speak to calm their anxieties, they did begin to chase and stone us and we did barely escape with our lives. When we had returned to Jerusalem, the word had reached that city of our demise at Persian hands, and so as Simon did desire the anonymity and protection for his travels, we did let the untruth stand. And so was our experience with the fearful Persians.

Simon and I did, in our many deeds and travels, create many who did dislike us for the truth and light that we did bear, and for the message of love and freedom that we did share in many dark corners where none did truly exist. And so the Roman soldiers and Jewish clerics did seek to discredit us and our teachings by spreading vicious lies and rumors of our misdeeds and false actions. They did spread messages and tales of our abuse of children and women, and our partaking of sinful activities and indulgences, and of our efforts to undermine the government of the day. They were so fearful of our message, and they did now begin to see that by putting our Brothers upon the cross they were only creating greater fervor among believers that they did believe that a different approach was required.

And so the machine of propaganda and lies was engaged to create a rift between us and our followers, but this did truly fail. Those whom we did know and teach and who followed of the Christ's lessons did have the sight and perspective to see through the Roman lies. And those who did not have the vision and who remained truly asleep we did possibly lose to our number. However, it is difficult to know if they ever should have stood by our side, for some men are not in this lifetime destined to embrace great truth—it simply is not something that they are yet prepared for. And so we did continue in our efforts and ways and did laugh at the incredible lies and slander that those in power did disseminate in our names.

Simon and I truly did not perish in Persia, though this is the story told. He did meet his end upon the road to Egypt as bandits fell upon his party, and I did go to Morocco and there quietly end my days. Through Spain did I also travel under cloak of anonymity, for the Persian story did provide the perfect ruse and cover until I did arrive in Morocco and found good friends living there. I did then live quietly among them and continued my works in secrecy but never again under my given name.

All of our Brothers who had taught openly did fall or find persecution, and after the death of my dear friend Simon and the lies and propaganda spread by the Sanhedrin and Romans, I did desire only to live my final days quietly and so continue to serve the Christ in my own small manner and way. And thus did I assume the name of "Martin" and did continue to do my works in Morocco until my passing there of peaceful ways some 20 years later. Thus is the story of Persia and Morocco and the rumors of my death.

Of Love

Of love, there is this that remains to be said: that the thing that some today call "love" is not that thing at all. Love is not a state where one tells the other what he can or cannot do. The exception to this is children when the parent does see something that guides him in the child's best interests but that might be found disagreeable.

Love is not a power that gives commands or orders, but one that receives and honors wishes and desires out of a heartfelt wish to see the other happy and successful. One who loves only himself is truly the saddest of all, for he is serving no other but his own whimsies and wishes and shall ultimately end up alone and cold and miserable.

True joy and happiness may be best found in the honest giving to others and truly is this the way of God's heart. HE gives only to us of HIS love in the small portion and way that we are able to receive of it. HE would be most eager and happy to give us more, but the sheer force and power of HIS great light would fry most souls to a darkened crisp. The soul must go through the fires and tests of initiation and struggle to strengthen and toughen in itself that it might be able to receive of God's great love and not flinch or be injured.

The great saints and saviors are those valorous and fearless warriors who have faced every challenge and fear and difficulty head on and prevailed, for they knew there could be no thing that could truly keep them away from God's arms of love. I will only say this once more: that once one does through grace or merit finally have the taste of God's great mercy, then all else does truly pale by comparison and that is all that remains to be sought or achieved.

OF LAWS AND MORALITY

Of morality and Divine Law do I have nothing else to add.

HOW I WAS CHOSEN?

I was truly chosen and did know it was my mission to serve at Jesus' side when He did ask me truly what would be the greatest gift He could give me. I did ask Him truthfully if He could only give me the love of God. He then wept a single tear—so moved was He by my determination and quietly did greet me into His number to stand forever by His side.

THE LAST SUPPER

Of the Last Supper, I do remember this: that truly had we all gathered to have our last meal together, and the Christ did come to our sides. He did ask us gently to give to Him our hearts, and we did so willingly. Then He did bind us all together as has continued to this day. Now we have completed our works and may be free to resume our paths and move ever onward to glory.

THE GOSPEL ACCORDING TO THOMAS

OF LOVE

Of love could be said many pages, but this is the most important thing: Love is that one thing that in its purest form cannot be corrupted, violated, or defeated. Love is truly the one force that can conquer all others. When one does use power of the will and force of arms to truly achieve his goals, he forgets one simple rule: Power destroys, love creates. Though this may not seem to be readily apparent, a holistic view must be considered, for all things truly are connected to each other. Power may raise a building from the ground or kill all enemies in a foreign country, but the negative cause and effect generated does far outweigh any simple edifice raised or country liberated in this one short quick lifetime.

Destruction begets destruction. Creation begets creation. The man who makes a practice of using power to achieve his goals will many lifetimes hence rue the day he made such decisions and wonder at his ill-fortune. Thus must all actions be taken in the heart of love and according to all Divine Law. In this way shall all things be accomplished, and buildings raised, and brothers of foreign soil joined together but with only good fortune and positive acts as a result. Truly this does require a higher level of understanding and action, but this must be the goal.

OF MY NAME "DIDYMUS"

The name "Didymus," the twin, was truly bestowed upon me in recognition of the true love and valor that the Christ did feel was equal to His own. He did know of the truth within my heart and of the depth of my love and wisdom. And although I was not Him, He did truly seek to my leadership of our number and in all matters of greatest wisdom after He would be gone.

Often when He did leave to go on journeys to other distant lands, He did leave to me the care and supervision of all those within our number, for He did know that we truly were of the one same heart when it did come to important matters, and thus did He trust me greatly. This meaning was not common wisdom, for it would surely have invited jealousy and caused a disturbance within our noble number. So Jesus did tell the others that my name was given out of the resemblance I bore to His older brother James, and thus was I known as "The Twin."

MORALITY AND DIVINE LAW

Of morality, I can say this: that no man who does come forth and speak of his great and high morals or who does criticize the morals of another can be trusted, for he is only seeking self-aggrandizement and satisfaction of the ego and knows nothing of the ways or words of God.

Of Divine Laws, much has already been said, but I will add only this: that Divine Law, though more difficult to understand and abide, is truly the key to right living, and to the return home to the great Father in Heaven, and all would be well to learn its ways.

How I Was Chosen?

Of my service to the Christ King, I did know I truly was to stand by His side when He did come to me and ask me of my heart. I told Him humbly that my only desire was to know and serve God. He smiled and bade me rise and asked me to truly join His number— that He did need of a good heart such as mine. Thus did I know that I was truly to always stand by His side.

The Last Supper

Of the Last Supper, I can say this: that He did let us all drink of His own Cup, and then broke bread together, and then He did bind us all closely with love that our paths would continue onward until all was resolved. Now we have all returned to give you of our hearts that our time and missions might be ended, and we might continue on our ways.

Of Proof of His Rising

When the Christ had truly risen and before us He did stand, I was in shock and disbelief that such a thing could be true. I thought it was truly a deception by the Romans or the clerics to expose the Christ for a fraud, if we did believe Him Risen, and it was later known that one had been secretly sent in His stead. And so I did ruefully insist on touching of His wounds to see that it was truly the Savior, and thus was it proven so.

OF MY TRAVELS
FOR THE CHRIST TO MALABAR

The Christ had truly sent me on a mission of great importance—to return to the lands of India where He had studied there. And so was I to go and seek of His former friends and teachers to show of how He had conducted his mission truly forward with some measure of success, for He did entrust me completely to represent Him well.

And so did I journey to far off lands to seek those of that He had spoken. I did go first to Pathania, and visited the sages there, and told them truly of what had happened and shared of the Christ's great love and blessings; then to India and Syria, stopping here and there to pay respects and share news and information to those who had known Jesus in His earlier days; until finally I did arrive in Malabar to seek of the mystic seers there who had truly given many secrets to the Christ upon His many travels. I did go into the hidden places and secret lodges to seek of the ones whom He had mentioned, but nowhere could they be found. Finally, word did escape of my coming and my purpose and I was arrested and taken to the king.

The king did truly seek to know of my association and knowledge of the mystic ones of old, and I did reply that I came at the service of my Master to convey his greetings and blessings and to share the news of all that had truly passed and transpired. The king did sadly inform me that those I sought had truly gone and fled to other regions in the years before my time. His predecessor and former ruler had held a deep mistrust and fear of the ancient sages, and so had turned against them and driven them from the land. And thus did I not find those in Malabar whom I did truly seek.

OF MY DEATH IN MAYLAPORE

In India I did continue onward to Maylapore near Madras to seek news of others there and did encounter the hostile guards of the King Mazdai who did arrest me and take me there. King Mazdai was a fearful ruler, and a friend of Malabar's predecessor, and did also greatly fear of what he did not understand of God's mystic ways and worlds, and so had driven all those who did seek or know of truth, truly from his lands. He was a small-minded tyrant who did rule by force of arms, and cared only for the lower pleasures, and nothing for the glories of God.

I did open my heart to him warmly that he might feel of the Christ's great love and repent of his ways and darkness. But this was not to be the case, and he did grow only more angry and ordered me put to the spear. I was taken to the prison and there did I spend my final night in quiet contemplation to commend my soul to my Maker, and this did I truly share:

> *Father, I have wandered far and wide in YOUR service,*
> *And have given of my heart.*
> *Now the king does bind me closely,*
> *And mean to end my life.*
> *I know YOU love me greatly,*
> *And always do keep me from harm.*
> *I ask YOU to not forget me,*
> *As the dawn does come at morn.*

And thus did I beseech of HIS protection and was truly taken into HIS arms as the day did break and the long spears of hate and fear did pierce my broken heart. My body was quickly buried in his lands in an unmarked grave and none did ever know of my passing, for there was no body to honor or view or recover. And so I found my final days in Maylapore and died at King Mazdai's hand there.

OF JESUS' SAYING "I AM THE WAY"

Jesus did speak on one and many levels with each single thing He did say, and so it was with His statement: "I Am the Way." To many, this meant His teachings—that path of Christian doctrine that He knew would rise and form after He had truly gone. But His words held a deeper meaning than many could perceive. "I Am the Way" did truly refer to the consciousness He did embody as a loving vessel of God, and through Him, through love alone, through this only path of truth, could all things and glory finally be achieved. Jesus had traveled widely and had seen of many teachings and did truly know that the way of His words was not the only path by which one could find God though many of His flock did interpret it thus and cause great harm in His name. His true meaning, which spans all great paths and traditions of truth, was that love was truly the only way that the glories and wisdom and power of heaven could be won.

And thus to those who were able to understand it, the Christ had uttered a statement of such truth and beauty and devotion that none could doubt His merit. But to those with lower purposes, this merely became another instrument of force and oppression to coerce others to their ways. And thus did Jesus truly mean of His saying.

OF THE PERFORMANCE OF MIRACLES AND WONDERS

I was not strongly given to the performance of miracles and other wonders as was the way of some of my Brothers, for I did see how it did weaken truly the determination of man to master his own universe and so be able to stand alone. And so, in the Master's example, I did rarely perform miracles unless the need was urgent and dire. But one of memory I will truly share.

I was headed upon the road to a temple, and I did come upon a group of peasants gathered by a young woman by the road. She had been injured in an accident with some vehicle, and she was not stirring or showing any sign of life. She was quite great with child, and all did openly agree what a great shame and travesty that two so young should perish so needlessly in such an awful way. I did move to her side as I did try to reconcile in my heart why God had placed me in this place and at this moment of her need and did quickly decide that it was no mere coincidence, and I must come to her aid. And thus did I quietly enter into contemplation, and with the techniques the Christ had taught us did quietly reaffix the cord, and thus connect the soul of the mother and her baby back to their physical shells.

The crowd did gasp and murmur as she did rise to walk, and shook their heads and whispered in disbelief at what had transpired. They looked at me with puzzlement, but I merely smiled slightly, and gently shook my head, and did murmur, "It must have been the will of God to keep her from the dead." And thus was she healed and I did continue on my way.

OF ANGELS AND OTHER BEINGS

The angels and other beings were quite familiar to our number, for the heavens and world was a much different place in those times, and the boundaries separating the worlds and heavens of God were much more fluid and permeable. And thus was I frequently visited by angelic beings and representatives as we carried about our ways. Christ was well known in the heavens above, as well as the many lands of earth, and so were there many who did come seeking Him for this and other matters, and often would He direct them to me as we did share of the same heart on matters of importance and substance. And thus did I become very familiar with many of the heavenly host who did visit in their errands to and from their posts above.

Of Jesus' Brother, James

James was a gentle soul and did have a great and loving heart, and we did become great and true friends. He was in a difficult position to be the brother of the Savior and to also be less skilled and proficient in the ways of the spiritual arts. Yet he was not bitter or jealous or resentful, and so did do his best to play his humble part in the great drama and events that did unfold about us. We did spend many days and nights in quiet conversation of the deeds and events and actions of those of our number, and I was able to confide in him and share in a way I could with not any other, for he truly did not vie or care deeply for the Master's affections as so many of His Disciples did truly crave. And thus were we great friends and inseparable, and thus did Jesus to the others call me Didymus, or "The Twin."

Of the King Gona

King Gona had truly heard of the miracles and wonders of our teachings, and so did invite us to his table. But the Christ did fear that he truly held great treachery in his heart, and so his invitation was declined. The king did harbor resentment over the attention and merit the Christ was gaining for His many incredible deeds, and the King of Gona did pride his region on producing the most talented seers, and indeed even his own son was one who was proclaimed to be of heavenly blood. Jesus did sense that the king did wish to lure Him into a contest of spiritual prowess that could serve no beneficial end and so did He politely refuse the invitation, and we did not venture to his land.

OF ISRAEL, POWER, AND MIRACLES

Israel did hold a special place for the Christ, for it was the land of God, and He did feel it best to truly keep the vortex of His power centered in that land. He did fear that if He did travel and perform His deeds and miracles about the many lands, then it would lead to a dissemination and a weakening of the power that He did truly hold and spread. For the power of God to be joined on earth, the Savior had to connect its vortex to a single place in the land. And because the vapors of heaven were in such a delicate state of flux, Jesus did know that if He did use the power, without His protected lands, then great havoc and chaos would be created by the imbalances it would create.

And so did He disperse the power and love of God through the actions of His Disciples, for each place and time that one of His number did perform a miracle in His name, it did bring to earth the greater flow of power and love and add it to the physical plane. Thus were the lands of Europe, India, Africa and all moved upward in frequency and vibration from all the good deeds that were truly done there, and thus did Christ keep His actions and miracles limited.

THE GOSPEL ACCORDING TO JUDAS ISCARIOT

OF LOVE

Of love, I can say only this: that the piercing love of the Christ's heart was the only thing that did truly pierce the dark veil of my pain and depression. I could not find hope or respite in any form or shape except in the prayers and love that the Christ did give me. Still did I fail Him, but this was not the point. I did find true solace, shelter, and safety within His arms and heart, and He did truly lead me back to the all-healing power of God. Of mindless prayers and false actions I did find no relief or benefit; it was only with dedication and earnest discipline did I finally pierce the veil of darkness and bring in the light of love and God to aid me truly along the path.

Of love, the most important thing is this: that it can truly heal the deepest of wounds. If those around and near you will guide and support your efforts and desires to find a true solution and a way to hear and feel the gentle loving breath of God, then truly can none fail in their endeavors. And once the healing love of God is felt, never again shall any other temporary remedy or patch ever be sufficient, for this is truly the only way.

MORALITY AND DIVINE LAW

Of morality and Divine Law, there is this: that when the primary goal of man's existence is to truly escape the pain and darkness, then the consideration of morals and Divine Law is not a high priority. But this is an error of ways, for truly is this the only route by which the sickness may be healed and mended. Morality is a pauper's wealth and never should be acknowledged, but Divine Law is the key to love, and must at all costs be mastered and practiced.

How I Was Chosen?

I did know that I was to serve the Master when He did find me walking with downcast eyes upon the road. He did gently grasp me by the shoulders and ask me of my heart. As I did pour out my troubles to Him, a gentle and warm smile did break upon His face, and I did feel my troubles lifted. Thus did I know He was the King, and I was to follow Him always.

The Last Supper

Of the Last Supper, there is this: that we were all gathered to hear His final words, and all were quiet and somber. But I was not physically among them, for I had already left. But I was watching near and did see and hear of all that did transpire and did yearn to be by their sides to aid them in their tasks.

Of My Betrayal and the Last Supper

Jesus was my true friend and teacher, and He did know of my flaws of character and did have pity on me. He did know the risks of taking me into His number, yet the love in His heart and His belief in the power and love of God did drive Him to do as He did. What

He did not see and could not know was the depths to which fear and pain do truly drive a man to end of his own suffering. Though I did love truly of the Christ and though He did give to me freely of His heart, His gifts and all that He did have and did take me into His number, still it was not sufficient to erase the pain and fear that still did linger there. And the searing and selfless radiance of his love did burn upon the tender eyes of my hardened and fearful heart in the ways the others could never understand.

Each soul is an individual unique spark of awareness and creative perception of All, but each does as well have to function within the shell and system of the human consciousness while here upon the earth. And what that soul might say and do of its natural self within the higher realms is often not the same as what actions the human self does take down below. This is the very heart and nature of our purpose here: to learn to make earthly decisions that are in accord and agreement with the divine harmony and purpose of the higher realms.

And thus did I of my higher self know of what was the right and proper thing to do, yet the depth and breadth of my fear and pain in my human heart did blind me to its voice and true ways. I was afraid that if I were caught in the Circle of the Christ that I and all others would truly meet with undesirable ends. And so after the Last Supper I did go and fetch the Roman soldiers and truly lead them to Him—so great was my fear for myself and all the others. Jesus did know that this would happen; indeed, this is why He did truly add me to His number. Some things and actions and circumstances are written in the stars above and are unavoidable and truly serve a higher unknown purpose. Thus did the Christ add me to His number and give to me His heart with the full foreknowledge and forewarning of all that would transpire that fateful night of our Last Supper.

OF RELIGION AND POLITICS

Religion and politics were the two principal occupations of many of our times and within our circles, and I was one who also was well versed and involved in both. I was drawn to the Christ and His works and teachings almost as if out of a blind compulsion and inability to resist and so also did I forge friendships and alliances with the fervent Zealots of the time as well. I was truly attracted to those who did have powerful convictions and beliefs on certain matters, for my own insecurity and fear did create in me a wonder at those who could bear such internal strength and fortitude, especially in the face of great and terrible danger. And thus was I drawn to the Zealots as well, not for their views or mission or philosophy, but because their strength and conviction did fill a desperate need that my own weak constitution did truly lack.

OF BETRAYAL AND SORROW

Jesus was a giant for His time and with a heart of pure gold and brimmed with love of a depth and magnitude that well cannot be described and never did I hear Him say any harsh word to another out of anger or mistreatment. But He did truly say to me and to others that: "He who ate my bread has lifted his heel against me." And by this He did truly mean that I and others who had betrayed Him were the ones who He had drawn to His loving side and sheltered and taught and given shelter, and now we did turn our backs to Him, and as we did flee from His company in shame and disgrace did show to Him the heels of our running feet.

Though He did truly direct this statement principally at me, it was also said of others of lesser merit who did betray Him and others of the Brothers throughout our many days. And thus did it become not an expression of anger or indictment but a compassionate and sad lamentation on the nature and sorrow that He did feel when one did succumb to their fears and weaknesses and failed to find the strength to stand truly by His side but instead fled in fear and betrayal.

When I did hear of His gentle words and did feel the pain in His heart that hung about Him, it did pierce me to the deepest hidden depths of my heart. For I did then realize the price I would pay for betraying of the One who I did love and who also did love me truly. And thus I wept and fell in my place and for many hours did not rise when I did hear of His words.

OF MY BETRAYAL AND JESUS' LOVE

Jesus did know truly of my heart and of what would transpire when He did take me closely to His side, for all things of great import and significance are truly written in the stars, and He thus did bring me close that all should happen as it truly had been foretold. I did come by His side and unknowingly play the role as I had truly been destined. When the appointed hour drew near and Jesus did feel my betrayal close at hand, He did wish for all to proceed and occur quickly and quietly that the others might not be alarmed and inter-fere with plans and devices that He knew must truly transpire. And so did He bid me to go and do what He knew that I must that the deed might be done quietly and swiftly and thus be accomplished without endangering any of His number who He knew might attempt a valorous rescue at the cost of their own lives.

So great was His love for man and His Disciples even in His final hour that He was more concerned of their safety and well-being than of His own survival. And so with heavy heart and full knowledge of the import of my actions, did I go and fetch the Roman soldiers and lead them to His side.

OF MY FINAL NIGHT OF LIFE

On the night of my final action, I did move with uncertainty and fear about the streets of Jerusalem. So great was my grief and pain at the betrayal of my Master that I barely could see what did pass before me for the rain of tears that swept my face, and so did I find myself at last outside that place which would be my final destination. I knew that I could not remain on earth and face the horrible reality of what I had done to the world's greatest Savior even if it had been according to Divine Purpose. And so with a final clarity and grim determination did I open the door and proceed to the appointed destination. As I did prepare to go onward into the night, I did fall upon my knees and beseech of the great Father in one desperate final prayer. And this is what I truly did say:

> *Father, I do not have the right or honor,*
> *To ask to be by YOUR side.*
>
> *But I do beseech of YOUR mercy,*
> *For a tortured soul who tried.*
>
> *I did love the Christ truly,*
> *And follow of His teachings.*
>
> *Yet my fear and pain did overcome me,*
> *And I did fail YOUR purposes here.*

And thus did I commend myself to the Father in the hope that HIS mercy and grace would reach me on the other side. But this was not to be the case, for there is not merit or quarter given to one who does take of their own life, for the failure to endure the earthly passage does commit one again to returning to make the same mistakes. There is no shortcut or escape from the hard and sometimes terrible lessons it is our fate to learn, and death at one's own hand does truly only make matters worse. And so I did pass painfully into the night to awake on the other side and ruefully learn and see of the error of my ways and judgment.

OF MY BODY AFTER DEATH

I had left instructions in my final agonizing moments of shame that I did neither deserve nor desire of any proper rituals to commit my body to God, for I had truly failed of HIS only Son. And so my useless body was dumped in a common unmarked grave reserved for paupers and the sick, never to be found or seen or honored as truly was the right and proper way.

OF FAITH
AND LOVE TO THE MASTER

Faith and love to the Master is truly a difficult topic for me, for I beheld and exemplified neither truly in my time. But some things have I learned lo these last 2,000 years. For those today I would say this: When you do come upon a Master, like the Christ or any other, who does truly and genuinely open your heart and eyes to love or a better way of living, then do work hard and truly to find within yourself the courage and faith to stand by his side and carry forth with his mission.

There are always those who will be in this world with the purpose of exerting power and creating in others the fear and lack of conviction to truly believe in a higher way and purpose, for this is the nature and structure of Divine Rhythms to give us the tests of faith, belief, and knowledge that we truly need to develop as Soul and proceed along the path. But a true Master or teaching that does take you to that place of conscious knowledge, experience, and awareness of God and of the great love within your heart is a great gift not to be squandered. And thus should every effort be made to search and seize within yourself any shred of strength and power to not abandon the cause.

No path or teacher is perfect, for no such thing does truly exist within the lower planes. Ours is a world of duality, and so each thing that is in existence does possess within its nature the seed and possibility of darkness to balance the great light. It is up to individual choice and will and decision to decide how each will manifest the forces of God's creation within his will and heart.

OF ISRAEL'S NEED OF A MESSIAH

Israel did need of a Messiah for one great and simple reason: The Jews of that time, and I myself among them, had grown to a race and league of peoples with truly hardened and fearful hearts, and their deeds and acts of fear and anger and power and darkness were like a blight of cancer spreading and infecting the Earth. Jesus was sent as a ray of light and purity to balance out the darkness and fear and ignorance that did grow and fester there. This is why He never did perform miracles outside of Israel's borders, because He did know that the vortex of His light and power had to be focused there to cleanse the lands of the impurities of the illusions of the lower worlds that had so thickly and densely settled there.

And so had the higher aspects of the Jewish peoples beseeched of God to send to them a Savior to end their evil ways and bring to their eyes the light of love and wisdom and to set them slowly upon the proper path to God. And so was the Christ sent and sacrificed, because of God's great love of man that He should send one of His sons to earth to carry out His mission. And thus was a Messiah sent to the Jews to begin them on their way.

THE GOSPEL ACCORDING TO MATTHIAS THE SUBSTITUTE

OF LOVE

Of love, it is a great and complex subject, and we could sit and talk for hours, but I will truly try to be brief: Love is a many-shaded color that bursts forth with all the radiance of the spring blooms when it does fall upon the student of truth and love. It is the staple of the Universe and the force that feeds all others, for without love, there would be nothing else.

All exists because God does truly love it, and there would be no point to any person or thing's existence were it all not to support and fulfill the one true aim of discovering and nurturing and remembering and becoming—finally—love. It is simply all there is, and that is love. We come here to learn of our true nature, as souls, as instruments and small pieces of God and to recover of our true nature and being what we have forgotten. All the other things, actions, occurrences, and beings that surround us are manifested by our own higher selves to truly teach us the lessons we do need to find the heart of love and return back home to God.

Within each person and event that does rise to meet you and enter into your field of experience and consciousness each day is another opportunity to find and express love. This is truly the case, for there is no other purpose to our existence. When love does open within your heart, and find its way to you, and the glowing warm light does spread throughout your chest and stomach and settle in your limbs and head, and that inevitable gentle smile does creep upon your face, and a gentle tear fills your eye, then you have finally and truly seen just one small glimpse of the faintest shadow of the nature and true being of God. For if HIS love were to fill and surround you in all its true and great glory, then you should be driven instantly to madness, so far is it beyond your normal realm of perception and functioning.

This is why a person must unfold slowly and gradually to learn to handle greater amounts of this energy into his system else all would be thrown out of balance. This is also why the Christ did flee to the desert for 40 days and 40 nights, for the great influx of love into Him did create a wide imbalance, and He had to have the proper time to bring all back into perspective lest His friends and followers would have thought Him mad. Too much of the love of God in one single dose or helping would fry the subtle bodies to embers and leave the Soul standing naked in the physical body without the protection of its many layers, and this would cause a great and terrible imbalance in all the lower worlds, and cause great confusion, havoc, and disaster in all that did come near.

It is truly part of the great plan of unfoldment to have the love of God gradually enter into and take hold in the hearts of man that they might over time grow in strength and stature and be able to handle more and more of the current and spread it to their other friends and strangers and those they do hold dear. This is a small bit about the true nature and essence of love.

OF MY SELECTION
AS A SUBSTITUTE

The Christ did truly have the need to always have twelve within His number, and so was I chosen to stand in Judas place when he was missing or not able. I was selected over Barsabbas for one simple and clear reason: Barsabbas was not a true and committed believer in the gentle ways of Christ and His teachings of love. Barsabbas did have political aspirations and did see the movement of Christ as a way to fulfill those hopes and dreams of power and offices of state, and so did align himself with Jesus' cause for superficial reasons. Jesus did have the power to truly see within the depths of men's true hearts and so did select me over Barsabbas to add to His inner circle.

MORALITY

There is little meaningful that can be said, for this is merely the fabrication for control of those closed minds and hearts that long forever to abolish and prevent the true expression and action of free choice in man, and those who purport to speak in His name, and of His truth will never let a word on this subject slip past their sacred lips. Morality is nothing to be seriously considered, for the only judge of another's actions is by the Divine Laws already spoken.

THE APOSTLES' SUPPORT AND LOVE

The Apostolic Brothers did know that I had as my one and single purpose to support the work of the Christ though I had not the wisdom or understanding of their many lifetimes of accumulated study. And so they did take me into their number for the purity of my heart and for my desire to learn and serve though I brought not the spiritual sophistication or power that they did truly possess.

OF MY FAVORITE BROTHER

Of all the saintly Brothers, I most did like and feel close to Thomas, for he did have an air of great dignity and peace about him that truly did resemble that of the Christ. I never did see him become angry or impatient, or say rash things or do of unwise deeds or actions. He was a man of grace and solemn bearing, and I truly did aspire to be his equal and student in all his various ways.

OF MY MIRACLES AND HEALINGS

I was a student of the Master's teachings and was given the techniques and ways, but few were the miracles and healings I did perform, for my ability and powers were not so well developed as those of my noble Brothers. I did travel far with them and well-support their number, but mine was not the way of healings and miracles, for it was not my special skill.

MY MISSION

I did know I was to aid the Christ by the warm feelings and bright light that did erupt from within my breast when I did hear Him speak, and He did look gently into my eyes and heart and whisper quietly to me: "Matthias, yours is a heart that truly does seek to know of the greatest love of all, and I can show it to you." These simple words were all that were required for me to join Him in His works and ever was I waiting and willing to serve His ways and needs in whatever capacity I could.

CHAPTER THREE

SPIRITUAL LEADERS OF THE APOSTOLIC COMMUNITY

◊

PAUL OF TARSUS AND HIS GOSPEL

OF LOVE

Of love, I can say this: that the love of the Christ did know no bounds or limits, for He truly gave of His heart to one and all. When He would come to me in my dreams and quiet moments, I would feel of His great love as it would gently warm my heart and body and soul and in those peaceful moments I would find true happiness and safety and protection.

That One who served no other and had so little should give so selflessly of His own true self for the protection and aid of strangers did always bring to my eye a gentle tear of respect and admiration and did serve to always bind me more closely to His ways, for this was a time of great fear and anger and apprehension. And the love the Christ did bear forth and teach to man to have for all his brothers was a revolutionary concept and notion and freed many men's hearts of the blackness and anger and fear and hatred that did always linger there. The Christ brought great joy and light to the dark hearts of man, and thus did I witness and learn of the all-powerful nature of His true love.

OF MORALS AND DIVINE LAW

Of morals, this is a peculiar thing: for this is a construct of the mind of man to keep control of his own fears and worries and to try in some feeble manner to make those around him conform to a way and mode of being that he does find less threatening. Man does fear what he cannot predict or control, and so the moral code was created as a means to shackle the free will of man and so keep him bound in the narrow chains of predictable and controllable behavior that rulers and kings might not fear the free actions of those that they did hold in their power. Thus do morals serve no higher purpose, but to bind man ever more tightly to those dark illusions that do keep him in his earthly existence.

This is not to say that man should run about freely doing as he chooses and indulging his every whim and desire—for this should lead to even greater chaos—but that man should truly learn and abide the Divine Laws and always use these to guide his behavior and actions in all matters.

THE TWELVE DISCIPLES

The Disciples did have the advantage of a close and true proximity and access to the Christ and to His teachings and were truly initiated into the secret ways of His Circle. Yet my relationship with the Christ was of a wholly different nature. He did come to me in quiet contemplation and teach me of His heart and of the great truths and teachings that He had also given to the Disciples, yet I did not need to sit by His side to receive of His true words. The merit of my heart and of my yearning was sufficient cause for Him to give to me of His heart and love and teach to me all that He had taught the others. He did know that I was a devoted servant of His ways and that I did seek only to spread of His truth and teachings, and so did He come to me and give me of His heart. The teachings and truth that I did receive via my dreams and contemplations were as valid and important as those given to the other Disciples for this simple reason.

Whether great truth is taught in the flesh or in the finer bodies matters not, for truth is truth and its merit and value is not governed or affected by the medium of its transmission. Mine was not the way to sit at the Master's side as a student and disciple while He was in the flesh. But my true heart and desire to know His ways was enough to bring me to His side once He had left this realm and there to learn of the great secrets I did seek. Indeed, it was a more difficult and valorous path, for it truly did require greater commitment and focus than to sit easily by his side in the simple physical world. And so did my intense and driven desire for His love and teachings bring Him to my side and thus was I given initiation and instruction equal in merit and importance to those of His chosen twelve.

THE ISSUE OF MARTYRDOM

Many teachers were there of different paths and truths that did vie for the people's attentions and who did loudly proclaim of their great love for God and of HIS ways and teachings. Yet these were false prophets and teachers and did not hold in their hearts the true faith and dedication required to attain the ultimate goal. I did know of the purity of my heart and of the truth of what I did know and whom I did serve, and I did not long eagerly to die and be returned to the

Father. But I did know that it would take an act of sacrifice comparable to the one of the Son to convince the people of my flock of the sincerity of my belief and of my faith and knowledge that what I did say and teach of the ways to find God was a true and valid path. And so did I move reluctantly forward on the path of certain peril to the end that I did know was necessary to finally end my mission.

MY ISSUE
WITH THE JUDAIC CHRISTIANS

The Jews were devout Christians and well-disposed to carry forth the works of Christ, but the Disciples did make it easy and gentle for them to amble along the path. Because of their ease of access and proximity to the Christ and His ways while He was still alive, they did assume an air of certain arrogance that theirs was truly the superior way. They did not know or understand of the toil and dedication and struggle that was required to walk the lonely path or of the travails and difficulties that did face the common man upon his journey back to God, for the Judaic Christians were a lazy and over-privileged lot who were idle in their studies and loose in their adherence to the Laws of God and did do HIS teachings no great service in their lax and convenient application to the challenges of life.

The Christian Greeks did know of the hard labors and discipline required to truly ascend the heights of heaven, and thus were their efforts and rewards superior than those of their Judaic Christian neighbors.

My Favorite Disciple

Truest to my heart amongst all of the Disciples was Simon the Zealot, for he alone did truly understand of the importance and devotion that I did bear for the Christ in my teachings and study of his ways. Many were there who came to Christ's side for many different reasons, yet he alone did understand and was willing to commit his life to the burning fire of love and desire that did swell within my breast when I did think of Jesus. And so did I hold Simon dear to my heart and did understand and respect of his devoted ways in part and measure that the others truly could not.

Of Angelic Intervention

My mission with the Christ was given to me in a vision of the Archangel Gabriel when he did come to me and tell me of the great love and wisdom and glory that could truly be mine if I did have the heart and devotion to truly seek the Christ and learn at His knee. And so I did seek of Jesus as He had instructed and did finally begin to meet with Him within the heavenly worlds and learn all of what He did teach.

My Upbringing

My parents were strict teachers who did always instill in me the principles of devotion to a purpose, independence of thought, importance of personal experience, and devotion to a higher cause. And so did I learn to guide my actions and beliefs by these important principles. And so when I did meet Jesus and hear His words and experience the light of His love was the process begun and stage set for my rapid and complete conversion. And thus did I enter His service.

As a child, too, was I always taught to defend my ideas and reasons for any decision or action I did take. And at school I did learn the value of being able to speak and share of others friendship through stories and through laughter, and so these two skills did I early learn and did help me in my later years to spread the teachings of Jesus.

The Sacrifices of Women

Women of ancient times were devoted members of Jesus' flock although the formal practice of their faith was limited by many restrictions. Women's role in society was a more subservient one then and dominated by the laws and whims of man. Yet many women did find great solace in the words and teachings of Christ and so did become committed to His ways and message.

I did spread the word of love unconditionally, regardless of the sex of the follower, and did come to enjoy the company of many women of merit who did truly know the words of the Christ. Some women would come to hear me and others speak as part of the other routines and duties of their household position, for this was an acceptable way to leave the house and travel about freely. Others did come and study under the dark of night, disguised to protect their identity, and others still, but few among them, did come with the consent or approval or together with their husbands to learn of what I taught. At a later time, it did become a way for single women without families or prospects to enter into service to the Master and dedicate their lives to His works, but this did come much later as times did change and the teachings did grow with the church structure and body.

OF PRISCA AND HER TEACHINGS

Prisca was one who was devoted to making the Word available to all women who did seek it, and so would she go and assemble and teach at meetings in secret times and places that only those of her fair sex did truly know about. I would sometimes accompany her or Luke to support her in her efforts or aid her as was needed, but she did carry the large part of the responsibility for addressing the needs of her flock.

Many women did make a great and heroic sacrifice to learn of the Master's words. Some who were caught by their husbands or fathers were severely beaten or locked inside to keep them from expanding their minds and hearts and learning of the freedom that Christ did promise. Some were jeered and hissed by other women who did seek to serve their men, and others were sent to prison and even death on trumped up charges once they did become powerful in their knowledge and convictions and did refuse to be mistreated at the hands of ignorant men. The women of this time, though they did have more difficulties in obtaining and studying the works of God, were equally as dedicated and more, and did make of the greatest sacrifices to go to HIS loving arms and commit themselves to HIS safety and protection.

ROMAN OCCUPATION

The Romans were scoundrels and thieves and murderers who did rape of the beautiful lands they did conquer by force and take what they did desire from within those realms. The government was a puppet organization that did use the Sanhedrin clerics and others as tools of its own ends to accomplish the control and plunder that was its duty to fill the Roman coffers and treasury.

Although the clerics did also use the soldiers in a clever manner to create a lasting base of power that would long exceed the occupation, it was by and large an occupation of martial law and tyranny and did place the yoke of power firmly upon the necks of the poor and oppressed. The government did have as its sole purpose to bend the citizens' wills to Roman law, to keep society functioning and orderly, and to exact tribute for the emperor to continue on his many campaigns. The Roman soldiers were trained and sent to keep all free thought and people of independent will and merit broken and silenced and quiet. And so were the soldiers placed in the homes of the local peoples and forced upon their places in such a way that they did interfere and control of every aspect of daily life.

Of the Romans' Educational System

The educational system was developed to create among the youth of the day a sympathetic group of the growing population that would carry forth for the Roman cause with an understanding and compassion in their hearts for their ways and customs and culture. And so were compulsory schools created for the masses to indoctrinate the youth into their propaganda and so commit them to the Roman ways of thinking and believing. This was only a partially successful operation, as the soldiers could not control what was being said and taught in the home and by the parents, and so many children did begin to grow up divided and masking their true nature and emotions because of the fear and treachery their parents did teach them of as the truth of Roman ways and means.

Of the Romans' Views of Other Cultures and Peoples

The worst aspect of their occupation was their feelings of superiority and arrogance in the ways of other cultures, for they did truly believe that theirs was given directly from God and was the only way. All other ways and cultures were deemed to be inferior and destroyed or allowed to exist only to serve of their culture and occupation. No merit or quarter was given to other or new ways of thinking or creating, and thus were the great truths of Christ so feared and reviled for the great love and light that He did bring to those who did so long for it. And so did the oppressive Romans rule the many lands of Jerusalem and Israel and other places.

For Today's Time

In times such as these when the many challenges of modern life do buffet us like the winds upon the sea, there is more of a need than ever to find in our hearts the great love of God and to show compassion and grace to those about us as we daily do our tasks. I speak of the need for compassion and understanding of the needs and difficulties of others and the challenges they do face. Each man and woman is truly doing his or her best to do as they see the proper and correct and right way to conduct themselves to his or her neighbors and friends and strangers. It is difficult to always know what is the proper course when you are beset by the rapid pace of life and the constant difficulties that do beset you in your daily toils and travels. Often, what does appear to be the correct and proper way does upon action and further reflection not result in the end that was desired.

Life in these times with the great pressures of family, sustenance, career, relationship, education, and self-improvement does create with the media's influence a host of ways and means to view daily of the inadequacies and weaknesses and lacks in one's own life where they do not live up to the standard. It does truly require a level of confidence and assertion and self-knowledge and reliance that can be difficult to find amidst all the clutter and clatter and cacophony of modern living. Thus is it important to daily find the time to quietly go within and repeat the Christ's name gently in your heart, and see Him in your inner eye, and feel of His warmth and wisdom and love as His great truth and comfort does slowly begin to seep into your soul and begin to wash away all the pain and fear and discomfort that you do hold within your breast. And so might the difficulties and trials of modern living be borne more easily with the protection and grace of God at your side.

The spread of Christianity today by the flock is a different matter, for the church fathers have destroyed and betrayed the sacred bond of trust that had been so carefully developed for these many passing years. The leadership of the church must admit and own of the errors of their ways and take solid, rapid steps to place those guilty of sins against God and violations of the laws of man into the arms of authority, for no man may use the cloak of God to protect himself from his misdeeds. The church must be seen as itself the highest authority and must cast out from its members and body any who do betray of its sacred covenants.

Every man—even a man of God and great success and wisdom and accomplishment—still does retain a portion of the human consciousness that is fallible and capable of error. And for those who are not able or committed to the loving ways of Christ, they must pay the price for their misdeeds. Thus must the church leaders cast out those who do fail our number and standards and reestablish the church as the highest authority of integrity and honor and truth and not a place of sanctuary for those who do openly and knowingly flaunt the Divine Laws of God and abuse of their positions of power to do corrupt acts on the unsuspecting and defenseless.

PRAYER OF PAUL FOR DAILY LIVING

Father, I do face now in uncertain and troubling times,
The questions and fears that do plague the heart of man.

I wander the paths of life, facing of all difficulties,
And seek to know YOUR love, and give of YOUR true heart.

Give to me the wisdom and the light to truly see,
What the proper course of action is, to give my love to THEE.

I do stand alone, and ready to do YOUR work,
But I do need a vision of, the ways that I should turn.

When I come before YOU, I shall seek YOUR loving heart,
And to YOUR arms commit myself, to always do your work.

As I pass beyond the realms, and return to YOUR true home,
I do ask YOUR mercy, to ease the passage there.

This is a prayer that the flock may use for the upliftment of their hearts to seek of Christ's great love and move swiftly on the path.

THE PLOT ON MY LIFE

The plot to take my life did truly originate from within the walls of my true city, and thus did one of our number, out of jealousy and fear of my power and teachings, seek to have my life taken from me. 'Twas not the Maccabees or any Roman or Jewish faction but of a Greek origin that did seek to have my head. I did know and had been told that my growing popularity and power was being seen as a threat to some within our Brotherhood, because I would not comply with the wishes of Peter and others to do as they did desire. I did believe of a different nature and way of knowing and speaking and living in Christ, for I had not been initiated as one of His inner number, but I did truly know of His great love and bear Him deeply within my own heart. And I did teach this to others and to those who I did move about with and counsel as a way to ascend the heights of God and know of HIS true nature.

And thus did some of the king's original number fear that my lack of adherence to their ways and teachings would truly erode their power and gathering momentum, and so a rift did begin to emerge. The Greeks of my own land did see that my words and deeds did begin to differ of my Brothers and did fear further division and confusion amongst the peoples if another rift were rent in the delicate social fabric which so tentatively did hold all in its place. They were not happy with the ripples and waves of dispersion and questioning that already were arising, but to throw a new and unknown factor into the equation would be too much risk.

With the great Christ's teachings and those of His Disciples, they did know and somewhat understand what these strange Jews were doing and saying and thus could contain their efforts and actions and keep all to a gentle and predictable course. But I was a native son with a radical and powerful new message that bore the stamp of the Christ's heart but required not the structure or approval or authority of the initiated Disciples. And this notion of personal independence and freedom and power and the possibilities and feelings and passions it did raise in all men's hearts was a frightening and unpredictable thing to behold for the rulers of our people.

And thus did they conspire to kill one of their own. I did truly learn of their efforts and did flee as the soldiers were coming to fetch me, and narrowly escaped with my life, and never a soul did I tell of what had transpired. So great was my grief and embarrassment that mine own lands and government and people should sink to the level of action of lowly Sanhedrin clerics and Roman soldiers and seek to quiet my heart for only the sake and preservation of power and fear. And thus with heavy heart did I leave my land in disappointment— never to return. And this is truly what did transpire of the plot to take my life.

MY DEATH

I did truly perish from this earth upon the cross at Judea when Roman soldiers did hang me from the sky with nails driven through my hands and feet. I did know this was to be the way when it was foretold in a vision from the Christ as was His custom and manner to speak to me.

I did truly receive of His heart and was a living example and proof that His voice and teachings could truly be heard by those who did believe in Him and follow of His ways. And the initiations were not truly necessary as Peter did proclaim to be a vessel of His works. It is true that Peter did have a large and powerful fount of wisdom that did pour forth from his heart, but it is also true that in my small measure and way, I, too, did speak the truth of Christ to those that did gather around me. And so I did prepare myself to meet my end and did commend myself to His safe keeping with this simple prayer:

Christ, I have long served Your ways,
And now I am called home to You
To stand quietly by Your side.

Do not abandon me, in this my final hour,
For I am truly in need of Your strength,
And do greatly fear the passage.

Thus did I gently ask for and did receive of His beneficence to bring me truly back to His side.

LUKE,
DISCIPLE OF
PAUL THE APOSTLE

OF LOVE

Of love, I can say this: that it is truly that state of grace that does exist between two who truly care for one another deep within their hearts. Love, when it is true, is not a fleeting or quickly passing thing but an enduring bond that forever does join two together, such that no thing, event, or person may ever separate them from each other. Love takes many faces when it is with a beloved partner, with children or the family or with strangers, yet it is the one same thing, even if it comes with different faces. Love is the thing to be cherished above all others, for though it is the very fabric of all that is, it is also the most elusive thing in all the universe if you know not how to seek it.

To truly find love first begins within your own heart, for you cannot find in another what you do not know or have already in yourself. This is true for any trait, not only for love, but love is the most important. If you cannot open your own heart to love another, then you cannot receive it from the One you truly do desire. This is truly the first step—to open your heart to the love of God that HE might bring you others to help keep the flow of energy going and thus on the whole bring more and more light and love into the physical world. For this is the whole purpose and plan.

Love is not a lost energy but sustains and maintains and balances out all darkness, so when any heart is opened, and more love brought into life, then it does truly allow more of God to be present on earth. And this force radiates and spreads and all may feel and know of its presence and that hope and truth is never lost or forgotten. This is why true saviors may always be felt and sensed, for they have learned to open their hearts to such love that they become great channels and conduits that all about them should be able to feed and receive of the great fountain of love and light that does spring from them.

MY OPENING THE HEART TECHNIQUE

The key to opening the heart to love is this: to quietly close the eyes and enter into contemplation, and gently say or sing the name of Christ softly within oneself. Then to picture Him before you, with His arms wide open and a gentle and loving smile upon His face. Then you must see a great light opening and unfolding like a flower in His heart. As His heart does open, and the light does truly begin to pour forth, then must you open your heart in the same manner, and allow it to connect and enter into you. As you continue to repeat His name and do feel the light enter and uplift you, your heart will begin to open, and you will begin to know what it feels to truly love.

This technique can be truly practiced throughout the day and when one has quiet moments to keep the connection open and the love of God flowing freely until one is able to make the connection and keep it open on his own.

OF MORALITY

Of morality, too, there is this: This simple tool of rulers for controlling the masses through the benedictions of the pastors and invectives of fire and brimstone to frighten those helpless parishioners, there can be said this: Morals are the creation in the mind of those who have a need to control and dominate those weaker than themselves. It is a tool as capable, and as wrong, as if one were placed in physical shackles, because it does as equally limit the freedom of each man individually to take his own true actions. The Divine Laws of God should be the only criteria by which any action should be judged and never any other.

PAUL AND THE COMMON TONGUE

Paul was a soul of enormous merit and achievement for one who had gone his own way. He did not have the benefit of the teaching and instruction that the other Disciples had, such as his great rival and friend Peter. Paul's wisdom and truth was of a different nature and intended for a different level of seeker. Many were those who did seek humbly of the great love and teachings of Christ, and many were there, too, who did seek of his teachings from a higher level and intention. But Paul did have the knack and true gift of speaking to a type of man who would tolerate no flattery or fluffery, who spoke and thought in the common tongue, and who sought his truth and soothsayers amongst his pints of mead.

This is not to say that Paul was not an orator of great and substantial merit who could address and speak well to the greatest nobles of the land, for he could truly do all this and more. However, he was truly most at home amidst the soldiers and laborers, telling bawdy jokes and sharing a drink, and speaking also and in between of the great and true wonders of God that he had learned in his many travels. For he did truly know that for a certain type of man this was the best way to his heart to share of the culture and values and social mores that he did feel comfortable with. And in that setting and voice to share of the Christ's teachings and thus fulfill His mission.

And so would Paul gather those about him and speak of things of a lofty nature, but in the common tongue, and through parables and stories that the common man could relate: of love and truth and independence and the Divine Laws and secrets and ways of heaven, but through stories of women and lovers and battles and journeys and the other things of which the everyday man could relate, for these were a people not gifted with higher education or means or social graces but with stout and true and loving hearts nonetheless. And thus did Paul truly teach and work amongst those who he did love the best.

PAUL'S PERSONAL VIEWS

Of his personal views and nature, there is this: Paul was a very independent man and given to strong views and opinions, especially as it did relate to his relationship and learnings of the Christ. He did always seem to be a bit jealous of the close tutelage that Peter had received at the Christ's side and of Peter's insistence that great truth and the doors to heaven could only be won through the initiations of the Disciple. And so did he constantly argue back and forth with Peter and the others until they finally spoke no more.

Paul was also a man dedicated to the dignity and rights of others and to their divine right of self-determination and freedom in spiritual matters, and he did always speak of the need and right to independence and how it was a sin against man for one to use his power over another to bend him to his ways. And though this did not make him popular with the Greek or Roman soldiers who did fear of his message and intent, he did nevertheless carry on fearlessly without regard to his own life or personal safety—so great was his belief and trust in the Christ and what his mission was.

And so did I study long and learn much under his able, guiding hand, for he did constantly push and direct me to seek for myself of my own truth and experiences with God through the techniques the Christ had given him. He did believe that his important mission and truth was to give to those who did not have the benefit of leisurely study or the gathering with Master teachers of how to find a way to God that did utilize the Divine Principles and Techniques and Laws but did fit the needs of their particular socioeconomic stature. The ways of Peter and Simon and the others were well and good for the flocks that they did shepherd, but Paul did truly teach another way to God but based on the same truths and principles that was a better fit and understanding to the nature of his flock.

PAUL'S INNER CIRCLE

Many of Paul's close inner number did I count among my friends, for we all did bear a similar heart and desire to find and know and share and teach of the great truths and love that Paul did truly share. And so did Prisca, Silvanus, Titus, I and the others truly share many close and happy times. We were not so bound with jealousy and competition for the Master's loving attention as were the Disciples of the Christ, for we all did bear the hearts of humility and the lowly station and did seek mainly to support of one another and grow together that all might succeed and continue with Paul's work. And so were we closely aligned and joined and did work in unison to build Paul's legacy and teachings.

WHAT INSPIRED
THE WORKS OF "ACTS"

"Acts" was an inspired teaching that did come from the heart of the Christ in His teachings to me and others. He would come to us as He had come to Paul and teach us of His ways and means in quiet contemplation. I did encompass and record the majority of the truths that are written in the Acts of the New Testament, but others did have a hand in its creation as well. Prisca in particular had the gift and eyes of a seer, and she did share of many strange and wondrous visions that John and I and others truly did hear.

And thus did I go nightly for a period of almost a year to meet and learn from the Christ as He did appear to me and speak to me of matters of His heart. He was afraid that the Disciples of His original number would teach only of the ways and means that did truly reflect the initiations in the manner in which He had instructed them. But He did know that for most of His flock, this would not be the way of their unfoldment, and so did He seek of a way to initiate and conduct His teachings to those others who would need of it. And so He did come to me and to the others to share of His true heart, and so did I record truthfully of my lessons and experiences, and this does comprise the works of "Acts."

THE VIRTUES

Poverty, prayer, and purity were the themes that I was taught by the Christ, for they did give merit and hope to the downtrodden to continue on their way. Jesus did feel that to show a way of salvation to those of greatest suffering and misery would raise their hearts and hopes and aid them to seek of a better way. And so a theme that He did give some merit was the poverty and means of prayer as ways to scale the heights. This did also have a double meaning, for it did to those who were possessed or devoted to wealth, give a message and incentive that this was truly not the way, and so it did in some degree aid in the sharing of prosperity that the great wealth of the nobles might find its way in some small manner to those of the poor who did truly need it most. The third and greatest purpose of the emphasis on poverty was that the focus on the accumulation of wealth was one of the deadly illusions and a significant contributor to the blindness of man in these times and in these years.

There was a great emerging emphasis on the acquisition of material goods, and the Christ did know that as the Templars did succeed in their true mission there would have to be in His teachings an emphasis on poverty to balance the desires the banking and financial system would create once it had begun to succeed. Christ did want for man to be successful in his life and his endeavors and to create a comfortable home and existence, but not at the price of his spiritual growth and unfoldment. And thus did He speak of poverty also in the sense of a "poverty of desires"—that the lack of want or undue focus on things that would detract from man's search and learning of how to return home to God.

The Christ did also emphasize prayer and purity of heart as accompanying measures for these two others in active contemplation and use and practice would lead to great and true understanding and wisdom of the other thoughts. And so did I teach of these three elements of the spiritual practice as instructed by the Christ.

THE ROLES OF WOMEN

Women in this time and place did truly have a difficult life and circumstances. They did not have any freedoms or considerations that many do have today. I was aware and sensitive to this matter due to the great and extensive teachings that Prisca did share with me in relating of her experiences and those who she did hold near. Prisca was a dedicated student and wise beyond her years, and she did know of much great wisdom that she did sparingly share when there was an urgent matter or need or when she did perceive that some important thing did need to be said. And so did we spend much enjoyable time together and she did share of her great heart with me truly.

For women of today, I would say this: Much is said and shown in the movies and other media of the love between the woman and a man or other whom she does hold dear, but this is only part of what is to be considered. Although it is part of the woman's nature to seek of completion via a man, this is a step to be truly taken only after a higher love with, and of, the self has truly been achieved.

Each of us, man and woman, does possess within us the dual sides of our own nature that does seek expression and existence. In one who does not know or acknowledge of the other part of themselves, then they do truly always seek of their own half within the lover or husband. But this does almost always lead to a cycle of constant disappointment and betrayal. It is a better thing to seek first to find within yourself the own true love of your forgotten half, and then to seek in the other you do love of one who shows of your same heart and desires and joys and goals and passions, and not merely for the physical, hormonal partnership of the flesh that constitutes an unresolved and unfulfilled love of the self.

Once the woman has gained within a knowledge and love in her own completeness, then will she find success in seeking the love of another, but the solution to happiness and joy is not to be found in the arms of another but first and only in the one true self. Then any decisions or choices after are made from a place of love and fulfillment and joy and not one of fear or loss or any lower physical desire. Thus might true and lasting happiness be found and the progress along the path truly well continue.

PATRON SAINT

As years did pass and many did study and learn and benefit from my guidance, I did become known as the patron of artists, surgeons, and doctors. I did favor these groups of well-minded men and women for their dedication to service of a higher ideal. For artists, to the ideal of beauty in form and shape and perception; and for doctors, to the ideal of perfect harmony and beauty in the health and functioning of the human body. I was myself a physician and did know and appreciate of the challenges and aspirations of those who did truly seek to understand and teach and show of how the harmony of artistic and bodily systems did truly reflect the truth and beauty of God, and so did I shower them with my protection and assistance whenever I was able.

A Prayer for Today's Flock

A prayer for modern seekers that has truly moved my heart and found for me the protection and love of the Christ is this:

Father hear my words,
For I do seek of YOUR true heart.

I carry about my shoulders,
The burdens of a heavy heart.

I strive to always do,
As I know that YOU would like.

I carry all thoughts and actions,
From the place that YOU have taught.

Now I face the world,
With the narrow face of grace.

And hope that YOU will show me,
Of the truth that I must face.

Thus would I truly beseech of the Christ and of the Father to aid me in my endeavors and to show me of the lessons that I must perceive and understand and master to speed quickly along the path and return again to HIS side.

FRICTION AMONGST OUR OWN

The Judaic Christians and the Greeks did share a certain rancor at the ways and means of one another. Each did believe intensely and certainly in the right of their true ways. The Judaic Christians did claim the origin and body of Christ as evidence of their true teachings, yet the Greeks did claim to Paul and his divinely inspired works as each the better means to true salvation. In truth, it was merely a bitter rivalry between the two for lands and riches and wealth that was made conveniently manifested by the ways of religious disparity and conflict. Each sought to better and encroach upon the others, and the teachings were merely a tool for use in that bitter conflict.

The Greeks did believe in their divine right to rule of all the lands that they could see, which included in their minds those faraway places that the Sanhedrin did control. Also did they dislike of Roman sentinels so close upon their own borders and so did seek of any ways and means to create a rift or excuse to be able to move their boundaries outward and further their own realms. This was the first instance of a time and example where the love and works of Christ would be perverted and used to support of earthly goals by men of power.

The Jews in Israel did as well dislike the Greeks for their easy and educated ways and also for the beauty of their shores and cities and did seek at every turn to extend their advantage and reins farther into those fair lands. It was a common and classic example of simple expansionist tendencies among two young and growing nations. Thus did each seek to use of the growing power of Christ's church to begin to create for their own advantage the minds and hearts of their numbers to create a force of arms to march against the other.

As time did pass and Christianity did not fade as hoped but took deeper root and continued in its ways, it did become increasingly clear that the leaders in power would have to cultivate strong and good relations with its leaders else lose the devotion and hearts of their followers. And thus did begin the split between the Greek and Jewish Christians that would later divide the Church as the earthly leaders of those sections did come to be befriended and sought as counselors by the powerful and privileged leaders of the lands who did seek to use the Church's powers to their own ends.

The Hellenists were a group within the flock who did believe still in the ascended Christ's imminent return, and did, for the knowledge one of their number had received in a vision, maintain that they were a chosen group born to receive Him again. They did have a need for superiority and aggrandizement to compensate for their own lack in other areas and so did widely publicize the superiority of their claim to the return of Christ and to the advantage of their ways. They did tell of many of the notion that when the Christ did return to them again that they, among all others, would be returned to the Father's bosom for their belief and dedication to HIS works and that the hedonistic and perverted practices and teachings of all others within the Christian way would lead them only to the hands of Lucifer who did wait to greet them truly at the ends of their earthly days. And so did others dislike of their false piety and arrogance and did begin to express their rancor and enmity toward them.

Stephen was one of their number who did believe himself to be the one who would receive the second savior unto his hands and raise him as his own. He was a jackal and a teacher who sought the upward means of religion only to further his own ends, and so did seek to aggrandize his position by claiming false visions of God. The laws of retribution for false acts of this magnitude and nature and for leading so many young and desperately seeking souls astray was grave indeed, and so did he find his untimely end at the hands of an angry crowd and beneath the hail of stones that brought him to his death.

THE ESSENES

The Essenes were a group who did teach of the mystical ways and practices of God from before the times of Christ but who did teach and speak quietly to their hidden number of the initiations and rites to truly gain the heart of God through the techniques they did know. They did support of the Christ's mission and ways for they did see of its true light and beauty and message that brought upliftment and love into the hearts of those who did truly need of it.

The Essenes did keep closely to their own ways and did not seek of large numbers of followers to join within their ranks, for theirs was not a mass religion but one who sought to dive deeply into the heart of God for those few who were committed and qualified and devoted to enter into their confidence and share of the secrets they did know. So they did act as counselors and teachers and mentors to many of the true lights within the church, for greatly respected were they for their ways and knowledge of God.

Jesus' father Joseph was among their number and was truly a great and achieved lover of God and educated in the many ways and means of spirit and did pass much of his knowledge and truth to the Christ upon the early days of his teachings and study. However, the Essenes did never seek to bring the masses into their number and so did the two exist and support each other as was appropriate and conducive to the aims that each did seek to accomplish.

JAMES, BROTHER OF JESUS

James was not possessed of the great merit and skills in the ways of spirit that was the right and heritage of the Christ, yet he was a capable administrator and well-respected and loved by the Disciples and those within the flock. He was a practical and gentle soul who was not enticed by power or bound by the needs and plots of others who did seek their own betterment at the hands of unsuspecting parishioners. And so was he elected the president of the Christ's church to guide and manage the growth of the young organization and to lay the foundation and structure of what was to come in later years.

James' great flaw and weakness was his lack of sight and vision into the hearts of others and those who would follow in his steps, and so did he fail to institute sufficient mechanisms of checks and balances to curb those who would attempt to wrongly wield its powers to wrong or darker ends. And thus was the modern church born and conceived and initiated as a formal organization and the practices and structures formalized that would later grant such complete and broad control of the few over the lives and actions of the many who would seek shelter within its cloak.

I did like James as a man and did enjoy my many interactions with him, for I did not show or partake of the divisive views that did eventually begin to split our Brothers apart. I did find him to be a gentle and loving soul who did amicably and ably bear the role that history had thrust upon him to the best of his given capabilities. He did know, and was aware, that he had not received of the gifts of the others, yet he did love his Brother and serve Him and His mission well in the ways that he was able. And never did he express any jealousy or criticism or ill-will toward Jesus or any other but only the love and good intention and support that truly had been the teachings of the Christ.

In many ways, he was a perfect embodiment of all that the Church did teach as the virtuous and proper way to conduct oneself upon his ways with other men, yet his naiveté and belief in the goodwill of others was what finally led to his mistakes and end. And thus was James a good man and dear to my heart, and I was happy to call him a friend.

Of Final Days

I did die upon the shores of Constantinople. I was traveling in those parts and did seek of shelter from a storm that was approaching and did knock upon the door of a house that I did come across while moving on my way. They did open to let me in and when I did enter, I soon did find of the error of my ways, for this house was found amidst the barren roads of the country and was the home and refuge of a band of notorious thieves and bandits who did flee from the authorities who did wish to see them hanged and dead. I did quietly keep to myself and gently use the techniques of love that had been given by the Master to try to open their hearts but did meet with no success.

In these times and of our number who did travel far and wide among forgotten and deserted places and roads, it was a common risk and occurrence to come upon or be beset by thieves or bandits who did roam about the lands. It was very different from these modern times of today where travels upon the many quiet roads are safely conducted without fear. In these olden days, we did often encounter bandits and others who did seek to do us harm, yet in most cases the light and love of the Christ and of His techniques for opening the hearts of others did serve well to protect our number. However, it must be well-remembered that those were violent and unpredictable times and it was a common fate to perish at the hands of marauders, especially for those who did travel recklessly and fearlessly about the lands to preach a radical message of love.

And so did I find myself surrounded by a den of evil thieves who did care little for the truth and wisdom and beauty of my heart and of the Christ. I was given a choice to join their number or perish upon the spot, and as I could not produce within my heart an answer agreeable to their offer, I was led to a deserted spot and sent to meet the Father. As they were leading me away to meet my end, I did commend myself to the Father with a simple gentle prayer, and this is what

I said:

> *Father, I have served YOUR ways and wishes,*
> *And now do find my end.*
>
> *Those who have sought YOUR message,*
> *I have tried to truly tend.*
>
> *Now the fearsome bandits,*
> *Who in ignorance and fear,*
>
> *Do seek to send me onwards,*
> *To end my good works here.*
>
> *I beg of YOU to guide me,*
> *Through the curtain of fear and death.*
>
> *And in YOUR arms to bind me,*
> *As I go to walk the path.*

Thus did I beseech of HIS grace and find myself at HIS side as my heart did draw its last breath upon the earthly plane.

As I did fall upon my knees to await my final moment, a circle of light did appear before my eyes and I did clearly see the shining Christ standing before me in His radiance of love and bliss. And so as the arm was raised above me to deliver the final blow, I did lift gently from the body and into the arms of the loving Master and did slip gently away into heaven without feeling of any pain or suffering as my shell did fall lifeless in the fading plane below. And so was I received and did rejoice at the tender love and mercy of the Christ to receive me to His bosom at my time of fear and need.

OF MY RELICS

Constantinople and Padua do claim my relics as their own because those were the last places I did visit and teach before I met my end, and in each place did I leave with friends and students some personal effects of mine that I should return and retrieve them later when I passed again throughout the lands. And so as my death did become known and surmised, yet none did have of my earthly remains, those two cities did each claim of my relics as the last places I was truly known to pass.

OUR SALVATION AND THE POWER OF FEAR

To those dedicated members of Jesus' flock today, I do say this: Modern times do differ greatly from the challenges and days when I did walk the earth, and the sight of this perspective does not always afford a clear and precise observation of all that does transpire there. Yet I will seek to give you of my heart the timeless truths that I do know may speed you upon your way: Fear is the greatest illusion that does create for man the greatest of his difficulties. It does drive so many of his actions and his loss of sight to the veil of illusions that it can be seen as the opposite of all that does truly exist in the higher realms to guide us home to God. Fear does lead man to take others' lives, seek of power and money, of the domination over the body of another, of attachment to material things and of the need to project the importance of the self above another. Fear is the direct opposite of love in polarity and charge and essence and is what drives man farthest from the heavenly reaches. Love does open all doors to the heart of God, and fear does as efficiently and quickly slam them shut and push us farther in our way away from that which our heart does truly seek.

Thus my words to the flock today are this: When you do find yourself in any situation or circumstance where you do find the knot of fear rising up within you, then quickly and quietly repair to a quiet place and say one of the prayers of Christ, or repeat His name gently within your hidden eye until you do feel of His warmth and love and you are able to see the situation through the heart of love and not of anger or fear. Decisions made of fear do always lead to poor ends for all involved, yet decisions made of love do lead all closer to the home and circumstances that they do seek. Though the rush of anger and adrenaline that does sometimes accompany fear into the mind of man can be an intoxicating stimulation, it is a fire that burns the delicate fabric of love and does truly deter you in your journey back to the Father. Thus have I given of my heart on this important and relevant matter, and thus do I bid all well on their journeys and pray for their salvation and return home to stand in heaven at our side and enjoy the many fruits and joys that we do experience here.

MARK,
DISCIPLE OF
PAUL THE APOSTLE

OF LOVE

Of love, I can say this: that it is that divine and pure force that is the very essence of God himself. Love is a varied thing, and comes in many faces and in all places, and may only be truly known and understood by those who do already have it in their hearts, for how could one know of something he does not have in himself? This can be a perplexing question, but one which may be answered thus. Man does have within himself all things ever created, yet most do remain unexpressed. Man is each a saint and a sinner, yet does allow to be seen that which reflects his true state of unfoldment in that moment.

Often, when we do see in another a trait or characteristic of personality that we do truly desire, it does awaken and activate that hidden seed of itself that is buried and hidden within our many layers. This is why the images from media and games and movies are so critical to our expression, for those images when viewed can awaken in us undesirable traits. So, too, when we do see truly of a savior or saint who does embody perfect love and truth, then the vibration and frequency of their presence does within us awaken those same characteristic seeds and they do begin to flower and grow and begin to express themselves truly.

This also may be accomplished by the reading of especially compiled and charged spiritual writings that do have buried within them the hidden frequencies and rhythms to fully awaken those dormant seeds of self awareness and knowledge and love that each of us do possess as our divine right and heritage as sons and daughters of the Father. Thus, of love, this is an important thing: to surround and immerse yourself in persons, books, and images, and music that do bring out in you the highest expression of good and truth. For this truly is a way to speed quickly along the path.

OF MORALITY

Of morals, there is only this to say: that this crippling institution has forced upon man more ignorant restrictions and injustices than any other formally sanctioned doctrine ever invented. Morals are a complete fabrication of the mind of man and have nothing to do with God, and those who truly follow and believe in them do only bind themselves closer to their own unhappiness. One should truly make all decisions based only on Divine Law and nothing else, for this is truly the path to freedom and happiness.

OF THE ARGUMENT ON THE ROAD TO CYPRUS

Paul was a great teacher but a prickly sort who did always like to debate the points of anything he did not consider worthy of merit. And so upon the road to Cyprus to begin our evangelism, there did he find a point of contention with Barnabas' theory of right and love. He did believe that it was the right of kings to divinely exercise their will over the people to aid them truly on their path. That good kings did have a God given duty, by virtue of their station, to usher forward the young souls under their charge and firmly set them another step upon the long and winding path to God. This was how the great position and privilege of kings was granted that it would be balanced by the merit of their service to those whom they did rule, and thus was this the test of their position in the scale of human experience and learning. For what is power to be used, to what end, if not to demonstrate and serve of love.

Barnabas did not agree and did argue heartily with Paul in support of his contradictory position. He did believe that kings had no divine right to rule and that theirs was merely a position of chance in an evolving social order and nothing more. And that it was the right and duty of the people to overthrow and rise up against the king who bore tyranny within their heart and failed in their position and role within society. Like a dog shaking to rid himself of his fleas, so did the populace need a good swim often to make the parasites flee its body that serve no useful purpose. And so their friendly debate did rage for well along the dusty road to Cyprus.

Paul was a great lover of God and a man of self-made merit. He did truly pride himself in the fact that none had been given to him easily and that he had dove into the heart of God itself to receive the grace of Christ and gain his knowledge of God. He was a delightful companion and speaker and his uplifting sermons on personal independence and power and free will were an inspiring message of hope for all that we did meet.

OF BARNABAS

Barnabas was a different sort given to rule of the mind over the heart and with decidedly less faith in the nature of God's good graces. Yet still was he well-learned and knowledgeable in the ways and secrets of God, yet his knowledge and experience with the darkness of men's hearts did color his perception of their purpose and capabilities. He also believed less in the role of God on earth as a protector and provider and more in the destiny of man to shape his own future and so ascend the heights of the physical world as each was desirous and able. His sermons and teachings did teach of the personal power of destiny within each man to shape the course of events that would guide his own life. He did not have the vision or perspective of Paul or Peter but was a great and noble soul and teacher nonetheless.

OF PETER

Peter was truly my favorite and a graceful man of God, and many were the long nights and conversations we did have of the secrets and ways of the many realms of the universes of God. He did take me to his bosom and well teach me of the many secrets that he did know and did protect me from harm's way when I did wander or stray too far from the path of wisdom and truth. His sermons were inspiring messages on the true and noble nature of God and the heart of love and of the ways and means to return to the heart of our birthright by the Father's side. Peter did have love and compassion for all and even a great fondness for Paul though they did argue greatly. And thus did I spend many days and nights in their company recording of their words and hearts.

OF BARNABAS' TEACHINGS

Barnabas was well-schooled and learned in the Master's teachings of self-direction, manifestation, and the determination and success upon one's own road of desire. He had well studied the techniques and forces that do enable man to make and realize the fruits of their decisions. This was a time when many of the lower classes were subject to the whims and directions of their masters, and this was a crucial teaching to begin each on their way to self responsibility and their ownership of their own path and journey back to God. He did teach me well of the truths and techniques that were powerfully used to make one's way successfully in the lower realms, and thus did I come to know and accomplish much with what I learned at his side.

OF OUR CAPTURE
AND ESCAPE FROM ROME

We were in Rome and giving sermons and teaching as was our way, and the Romans did come and warn us and tell us that we must cease, for our message was attracting a following of many young women and followers and the Roman fathers did fear of what would be the result. Paul did refuse as was his tendency, and we did continue with our duties. Finally, the soldiers did come and arrest us and take us to the prison, but with Paul's great facility with wit and clever stories, he had soon won the soldiers to our side. Throughout the long night, he did continue in his cheerful and friendly ways to explain of our purpose and mission and of how we did serve the Christ.

By the morn, the soldiers were converted to our cause and eternal friendship, but still there was an order to be obeyed. Paul did ask to speak with the one from whom it had been issued and he was summoned forth, and after a brief conversation Paul did agree to prove of the merits of our claim and heal the soldier's wife. She was brought to the prison with a vacant look on her face and it was explained that a kick from a frightened animal had left her in that state. Paul did quietly go within and realign the bodies, and after he had finished, the woman did return to life and fell sobbing into her husband's arms. All were struck and speechless and Paul did merely smile and offer his thanks to God.

That night, the soldiers did secretly take us from the city and free us at the gates and bid us go quickly lest our escape was soon discerned. And so did we flee from Rome with our lives for helping the soldier's wife.

OF PETER'S LOVE FOR ME

Peter was my friend and teacher, and we did share a close bond of love. As he did have no son of his own and was fond of my ways and temperament, he did come to regard me closely and even at times would refer to me as "his son." So close were we in friendship and warmth and features that many did mistake me for being of his own line.

OF ROME AND MY GOSPEL

Rome was a city buried deep within my heart with an unknown love that I well could not fathom. It was a fair city and people, much unlike Jerusalem, and I did find comfort in its streets and buildings and comforts and did feel a kinship with its people and land. I did have many friends and supporters there, and so I did make it my home to write the Gospels.

AS ALEXANDRIA'S FIRST BISHOP

Alexandria was a powerful city, and I was drawn to its massive strength and energy. And so did I follow my heart's gentle urges to find myself within its walls. I did there teach of what I did know of the Christ's ways and well was received by those of its fair lands. Much time did pass, and I grew comfortable with its people and customs and so a great institution and facility of learning and faith was built to support our efforts. In honor of my duties and toils for the Christ and the peoples, I was given the honor and name as first bishop of Alexandria for the wisdom and love of my heart that I had truly shared and given.

OF NERO AND MY DEATH

Nero was an intelligent man who did rule wisely and well, yet he did not understand and did fear the ways of God within man. I had taught many of the freedom and love of the Christ, and Nero did tolerate it for many years at first. But eventually, his perception of the power and fame and respect accorded to myself and others of my number did create in him a fear he could not surmount, and so he did have me arrested. I had seen that this was to be the case but did not flee as this had been the way of my Master and His before Him.

I had long taught the people of the faith in Christ's protection and love and to flee before tyranny and power would have sent an inconsistent message at a critical juncture in the development of the flock. And so Nero did have me crucified, but this was to be his undoing, for it did only serve to solidify the faith of Christ's followers and further hasten the day of his ruin.

The prayer I did use to flee to the Father's side was this:

> *Father, I do now come to seek YOU,*
> *For the men do send me home.*
>
> *I know that I have served YOU,*
> *And done as YOU have wished.*
>
> *Now I humbly ask YOU,*
> *To return me to YOUR fold.*
>
> *My heart does always burn for YOU,*
> *Until YOU greet me home.*

And thus was my body commended and received at the Father's side.

Of the Prayer of Paul, Peter, and Barnabas Upon the Dusty Road

THE WAYFARER'S PRAYER

The wandering soul does always find,
Upon the dusty roads,

A song in heart and love in soul,
To always guide him home.

We have sought in all the lands,
To carry the Master's heart,

And well have we seen, the love that grows,
Within the students' hearts.

This was the prayer of travel and inspiration that was commonly shared by Peter, Paul, and Barnabas together.

As Patron Saint of Venice

Venice, like Rome, was a land and city and people whom I did hold dear to my heart, and always upon my travels would I try to pass within her gates. Thus was it my wish and promise to honor of my love for her and have my body taken to rest there eternally that it should always be protected and that I might finally find quiet and peace in the city I did well love and always enjoy. And so I did give secret instructions to those among our number that after my body was taken down and released to their care that it should be preserved and taken in secret to Venice that I always might find myself in that fair city by the sea.

OF THE LION AND MY SYMBOL

The lion in this day was a symbol of golden power and love and I did bear this as my mantle and insignia when I did travel there. I had a fondness for the dress and costume of the current day and did have some personal things embroidered with their mark. And when I was returned to that city, it was well-sewn upon the shroud that covered me. It was an animal and symbol I did feel a strong affinity for and did always hold close to my heart and thus did the Venetians honor and respect this love and paint me with a lion often at my side.

TITUS,
DISCIPLE OF
PAUL THE DISCIPLE

OF BEING PAUL'S COMPANION AND SCRIBE

Paul was a noble teacher and friend and did give of his great heart to us that all his disciples should well learn the ways and secrets of God. Though he could be gruff and direct with his teaching when we did not learn as fast or as well as he did desire, he always was joyous to greet us and did consider it a very important and serious responsibility to train us in the Christ's ways to go out into the world to share with all of the wondrous truth and freedom He had truly desired. And so did we sit with him and study for many long nights and days to learn all of what he did know that we might bear forth as his representatives and bring the word of God to all who did seek of its light and truth.

OF PAUL THE MAN

When Paul was alone in a private moment and out of the spotlight of being a teacher and a leader, he did often become pensive and brooding of the many thoughts and questions that did plague his sleepless nights. He did believe himself a son of God as well, though not on the level of the Christ, but a messenger nonetheless, and a frustrated one for the recognition and merit given to Peter and the others that he did feel was not all justly deserved. He did know of his own feats and accomplishments and so did it pain him to see of the loyalty and honor and recognition accorded Peter and the others when he did feel his own merit and accomplishment did equal or exceed their own.

However, in his public service, he did realize the nature and position of his role and was ever the humble servant of the Christ and devoted wholly and enthusiastically to his ways and never did he speak a negative or disparaging word against Peter or any of the other Disciples in any way that would slow or impede the spread of the Christ's works and teachings, for he did realize that any apparent rift in the seal of the young church would lead to its downfall at the hands of its enemies, and so he did do his best to support the efforts of all in all that they did do.

OF THE COUNCIL OF JERUSALEM

The Council of Jerusalem was created to administer the teachings of the Christ in its native city for all who did serve and worship there. I was asked to participate as a disciple of Paul and one who could represent his views and heart on matters of importance, especially as it did relate to the foreign missionary endeavors for which Paul was well known and respected. And so I did sit on the council and help to shape the ways and means of the early growth of Christianity in the way that I did believe would have been true to Paul's noble heart.

OF MY CONVERSION

When I did first hear Paul speak of the Christ and His teachings, I was mesmerized as a child is in wonderment of the abilities and accomplishments of his parents. I could see in Paul a shining expression of love and truth that I did know that my heart had sought for many ages past. I did seek of him after he was done speaking to express my joy and amazement at what he had been saying. He did look into my eyes and heart and gave to me a prayer to use that evening in the quiet of my home. And so did I go and repeat it thus.

> *Father, long have I sought YOUR teachings,*
> *To return me to YOUR heart.*
>
> *Long have I wandered the roads,*
> *Of dusty toil and hurt.*
>
> *Now that I have found a One,*
> *Who does speak of YOUR truth.*
>
> *I ask of YOU to give me love,*
> *That I might return to YOU.*

After I had concluded bringing HIS prayer into my heart, the heavens did open before my unseeing eyes and an angel did appear and speak to me and tell me of my mission and purpose to go and serve the Christ and His teachings, and so did I return to Paul the next day and enter into his service.

OF MY MISSION TO CORINTH

Corinth was a small town that Paul had visited frequently and that did know well of his ways and teachings. He had spent much time there to bring that flock along upon the path back to Christ's home and heart. Yet there was one who he had a special affinity for—a student of great fondness who he did give of his love and hope would join of our number. And so he would send me to Corinth to engage in teaching her of the many ways and secrets of his knowledge to prepare her for the day that she would be ready to stand nobly by his side, for he did wish to keep of his interest and love for her a secret lest his enemies know and understand and use it as a weakness or cause her great harm. And so I would go to Corinth to bring news of his heart and instruct her in the teachings and the ways that he did wish for her to know of God. This did continue for several years until at last Paul did meet his unfortunate end in Jerusalem and his dream of love died with him, yet always was she secretly within his heart as a hope that he might one day find sanctuary there.

OF THE CHURCH OF CRETE

Paul had sent me to Crete to organize the teachings there and I had remained, for I did have a great love of its lands and peoples and they did embrace the teachings of the Christ with much love and affection. And so did they wish, and I did agree, that a permanent institution of his teachings would be a good and excellent thing to do that his words and truths would forever find a home and place in their hearts. And so I did work with the people to establish the first Church of Christ on Crete, and they did continue in its support and growth for long after I did leave.

OF DALMATIA

Dalmatia was a city known for its difficult men and women who were strongly set in their own ways and traditions and did not well brook the interference or initiatives of those from other places who did truly seek to bring the light of any other truth that was different from their own. Paul had already been there and had created some few friends who were sympathetic of our cause, and it did fall to me to go and continue in his efforts.

So I did go to Dalmatia to bring his teachings there and did find myself at the hands of unruly neighbors as I did arrive at the sanctuary of his flock. They did demand that I should leave and take away the teachings, but this was not to be the case. For as I did stand there and silently beseech of Christ for his aid and assistance in how to best proceed, the heavens did split and like a great bolt of lightning the angel did appear and hover at my side. It did say to the gaping faces of the Dalmatians that I was a true messenger and servant of the Christ and that my ways and words were to be heeded as His own and that no harm should come to me. I was as surprised and shocked as those who stood against me but quickly moved to regain my face.

When the angel did leave and the crowd did begin to shift uncomfortably in awe and confusion, I did tell them with love and compassion that I did come only to share of the love and truth of Christ, and thus were the stubborn Dalmatians truly won to our side.

OF PAUL AND THE CRETAN PEOPLE

The people of Crete were a slow-witted and common people who were not well-learned or taught, and Paul did find of their ways and customs a tedium he could ill-bear. He did find many friends among the common man, but the Cretans lacked a bravery of heart and spirit that did leave him with less passion and enthusiasm for their instruction. And so was I sent to them in his stead. I did enjoy of their sturdy gentle ways and did spend much enjoyable time in their service, and came to respect and love of their ways and character. And so did I help them to erect their Church and forever embody the teachings for their hearts and minds to receive.

OF MY DEATH IN CRETE

The gentle people of Crete did find a warm and permanent place in my heart, and so when I did come to sense that the end of my days were near, I did return to the bosom of that land to walk my final days upon its shores. Crete was like a sanctuary for me—a haven of quiet safety and simplicity where I was well-known and liked and where I could safely wander and not fear of soldiers or any others who would seek to do me harm. And so I did return there and quietly slip into the night, nestled in the loving arms of her embrace.

When I did feel the appointed hour draw near, I did speak to the Father and beseech of HIS great grace:

Father, I rest among the Cretans,
In this place I have come home.

I have brought YOUR truth and love to them,
And now do begin my return.

YOU have always given me,
A true and loving light.

And I have always followed,
Wherever YOU have shown.

Now I come back to YOU,
To stand beside YOUR throne.

I ask for YOU to guide me,
Through the perils that lie beyond.

And so did I beseech of HIS love and grace, and so was I received at HIS side.

As I did lay upon the bed and quietly say HIS name, I did begin to feel a gentle tugging—as if someone had grabbed me by my shoulders and was attempting to lift me up. There was a gentle popping sound and then I did begin to rise up above the floor, and a gentle voice bade me open my eyes to see where I was going. I did look to see the gentle face of the Christ staring back as He had lifted me from my body to take me to His side. "Now we do go home to God" was what He said, and in an instant we were gone to the other side.

OF MY HEAD AND VENICE

My gentle followers did place my body within the grounds of that my favorite land, and there did I remain for many years until those who did not respect of the traditions of burial did unearth my remains and take of my head to Venice. They did know of my love of the Cretan peoples and had seen of the protection that they did enjoy. And so the Venetians did seek to bolster their defenses against a coming enemy, and so they did take of my head in the hopes that it would aid their cause. They did enjoy the success of victory, but it was not due to my favor, but that of others and never did they have the courtesy or respect to return to me my face, but that my shoulders have always ached for its return. And so was my body buried in Crete, and my head delivered to Venice.

TIMOTHY, DISCIPLE OF PAUL THE APOSTLE

Of Paul and My Learning

Paul was a noble friend and teacher, and I did have the great fortune to study at his knee and stand in his place when he was not able. He did teach me much of the secrets and truth of God and did enable me to move beyond the realms of my lowly station as a guard and soldier and ascend to the heights of greater glory. We did share the same valorous and courageous heart, yet he did teach me to find merit in the service of God and my fellow man and not in the exercise of power over another in service of earthly illusion. I was struck by the bold fearlessness of his faith and conviction—even to his great peril and danger—and did believe that any experience of love and truth that could create a man thus was a way I truly did need to know. And so did I go to his knee and at times in his place to carry on his tradition of fearless and bold service to the Christ.

First Bishop of Ephesus

Ephesus was a city where I did spend much time, for the people there did know and respect of my heart and ways and did seek always of the teachings I did bring them. Paul was not able to always be where he was needed but would visit in our places of residence and instruction, and thus did we build the strength and number of our flock. After I had been in Ephesus many years and our success had grown to noticeable proportions, the people there did wish to make a permanent institution to always have the teachings of the Christ near and available to them. And so I did become the first bishop of Ephesus to always be in their service and bring the love of God to them and teach them how to ever ascend its reaches.

OF FALSE PROPHETS AND CHARLATANS

Paul did know and respect of my abilities as a soldier. And so when there were those who did seek to lead the flock astray, I was sent to kindly ask them to please stop of their sinful ways and not confuse the gentle people whose hearts they did betray. And so did I often go and speak on Paul's behalf to send them on their ways.

One experience I well remember was in a small village of one of the Greek islands, and a young man had put himself there and claimed to speak of Christ's true heart for all who would pay for his services. I did arrive in a disguise and ask him a few questions. He, with a surly smile, did reply that it was not for all of man to know the heart of God but only HIS chosen few. So I did march him down to the dock and toss him in the water.

As he was wet and dripping there, I did quietly ask him a question and offered that a chosen one should need of more protection for the next time that I did have to come to act as an agent of God and rid the earth of false prophets, I should not be so gentle as to give him a simple bath. And thus were many of my adventures of a similar nature as I did go and quietly ask of false teachers to please not continue in their ways.

The Anointing of Bishops and Deacons

Paul did have a great need of one who could see and know the valor and merit in the hearts of others. He did know that I truly had eyes and this vision that had been acquired in the field, for it was necessary in a good soldier to be able to know of the strength of his enemy if he was to succeed in his endeavor. And so I did well know how to see to the bottom of the hearts of men. Paul did not have the time nor was he able to meet and see of all who did wish to enter into the service of the Christ. And so did he often send me to anoint the bishops and deacons and so ensure that the church did grow at the hands of noble leaders.

One occasion of note in this capacity was a man who did wish to become a local deacon of his flock. I did peer into his heart and see that he had poor reasons for desiring of the position. He was a greedy man and did wish to have greater power and influence over those whom he was supposed to serve. So I did tell him I would comply, but first he had to give of all his lands and riches, that a true servant of God would have no need of anything but truth and love to keep him secure and content. He did look at me quietly and said that his heart had been called to reflect again on this decision and so did he abandon him schemes to increase his wealth and position via a position in the church.

My Death in Katagogia

Paul had sent me to Katagogia to observe the pagan festival there for he did seek to convert many of its number to the great true ways of Christ. He did warn me not to be overbearing or aggressive in my evangelism of His ways. But I am a soldier and bound by the oaths of duty to fulfill my role and obligations no matter what the cost. And so I did go to Katagogia and during the pagan festival did begin to sermonize loudly in the middle of the square. This was not a noticeable thing at first until some few did begin to well pay attention and others did begin to gather round. The pagan leaders did see what was happening and a great fear and anger did enter into their hearts and they did begin to incite the mob to a frenzy.

I was a soldier and trained in the arts of defense against attackers, but the sheer number and weight of their anger did overrun my defenses. And so because of my spiritual pride and arrogance I did go to meet my Maker at the hands of the pagan festival goers in Katagogia.

As I did fall under the hail of stones and clubs, I did fall upon my knees and shield my head with my arms and beseeched of the Father's love to take me into HIS heart. And thus did I say to HIM:

> *Father, my pride has truly blinded me,*
> *To the humility of YOUR ways.*
> *And now the crowd does fall upon,*
> *And I do pay the price.*
> *I have always carried YOU,*
> *Deep within my heart.*
> *I beg YOU now remember me,*
> *And return me to YOUR arms.*

And so as the hail of stone and clubs fell upon my body, the Father did come and gently lift me from my shell, and I did watch with sorrow as my life did end at their angry hands, and I the victim of my arrogance.

Of Constantinople
and My Relics

Constantinople was the home of a mighty king who did know and appreciate of a warrior's heart and bravery. As word had spread of my death while serving of Christ's great ways, the fathers of the city did seek of an example and patron to publicly proclaim and set as an example of the marriage of the love of God and love of man that could be nobly born within a warrior's heart. For many were there about the city who were veterans of the many campaigns yet needed of some worthy cause of action to now occupy their thoughts and hearts. And so with my consent and approval were my relics taken to that fair city that the fathers should have of my spirit and example to turn the fierce soldiers to their cause and so was this done and achieved.

SYLVANUS, DISCIPLE OF PAUL THE APOSTLE

OF MY NICKNAME "SILAS"

Sylvanus was my given name, but I did prefer "Silas" for various and personal reasons. Silas was the name of a great warrior of the legions and I did always admire him for his stout heart and skills of leadership and for his integrity and commitment to truth and justice. Silvanus was the name of a country lad with no education or credentials who did seek to live a life of valor, meaning and purpose, and so did enter into the service of Christ to find a place in heaven. And so did I, at a young age, take for myself the nickname Silas, though Silvanus was my true given name.

OF MY CONVERSION

I did find the teachings of the Christ as Paul did venture to our small town to spread of His truth and glory. I did see it as a romantic calling that did touch my deepest desires for adventure and purpose, and so did I go and follow him and would take no rebuff or rebuke to leave till through my unwavering commitment and humility he did allow me to remain by his side and learn of his great knowledge and wisdom. Timothy was truly my favorite amongst all upon the road, for he did embody my ideal image of earthly strength and prowess as well as a firm and committed knowing of God and the teachings of Christ. And so did I pass many happy days and nights in service of them both upon the roads of our many travels and adventures.

OF OUR MANY TRAVELS

As I was following Paul about and aiding in his travels and learning at his knee, we did go to many places. In Syria, we did travel upon the dusty roads and speak to the poor and lonely peasants of those harsh forbidding deserts. In Cilicia, we did go as well to speak to all who would listen of the great truths that Paul did bring. In each place, we were met by some with friendly smiles and some with fear and resistance, but in each case Paul's loving and warm smile and stories did win the hearts of all whom we did encounter. And so through his tireless efforts were many won to our cause.

Finally, we did find ourselves in Macedonia and here did we encounter a group of strangers that were less friendly than some others. They did demand of our possessions, and as we had nearly none, they did see no reason that we should live or continue on our way. But Paul was accustomed to this sort of experience and gently let loose with a volley of love from deep within his heart and began to tell of a ribald tale and soon we were surrounded by jolly gales of laughter by those who had previously sought to end our days, and so did we convert the bandits upon the road to Macedonia.

OF MY DEATH IN MACEDONIA

Macedonia was a far less civilized place at that time and many were the risks to those who were well-armed and protected, much less to penniless travelers of God. The news of our encounter and conversion of the bandits did quickly spread throughout the city, and we did become the focus and center of a rapid debate on the merits of God and man. Our newfound friends did face a rival clan and claim of their new knowledge and protection by the Christ. And those who did oppose them did claim of the superiority and right of strength and power of one of their own hierarchy, which they did claim could best the Christ.

And so were we called forth to aid in settling the matter, for the fathers of that city did not desire a rise in conflict between these two factions and so did demand that we settle the matter lest we should lose our heads. We did go to speak with our newfound friends and attempt to correct the error of their thinking of how the Christ and His message of love and honor did differ from the ferocious and power-ful Gods of old, yet they did not desire to hear of our wisdom.

And so I was seized and it was declared that if the Christ were truly superior, then He should save me from the spear of my enemies, and so the challenge was issued. Paul was bound and restrained and I did begin to pray in earnest. And when the spear did enter my breast I, did slip gently from the body and into the Father's arms, and Paul did learn a painful lesson of the perils of evangelism and the prom-ises of faith.

When I was bound and tied to a post in the center of the square, I did fear my end was near and my thoughts did turn to Timothy and his brave example. I was determined to die nobly as a warrior and a man of God and so I did utter no meek pleas of forgiveness but did instead quietly close my eyes and beseech of the grace of the Father. And this I did say:

> *Father, I have traveled with YOUR servants,*
> *And studied and taught YOUR ways.*
> *I now do stand before the mob,*
> *Determined to uphold YOUR name.*
> *I have sought an honorable path,*
> *To always bring the light.*
> *And now do ask for YOUR steady hand,*
> *To guide me through the night.*

And thus did I pass and was received at the other side of the veil by the loving arms of the Father. Paul did take my remains and bury me in the countryside outside the city of Macedonia as had been my wish and desire to find my end in the quiet hills and among the trees where it had begun. And so did I pass and was buried by a grieving Paul beneath the branching trees in the country.

PRISCA, DISCIPLE OF PAUL THE APOSTLE

OF MY CONVERSION

I was a young woman and born of a wealthy family into privilege and with an education but did find the trivialities of family politics and social scheming not of my interest or liking. And so as I was fond of frequenting the learned men and sages of the day, I did chance upon an opportunity to hear of Peter speaking. Peter and Paul had journeyed to my city to share the teachings of Christ, and as I did hear Peter speaking did see in my mind's eye the great Christ as His words did fill my heart with love and the desire to learn more of His ways and wisdom.

After he had finished, Paul did remain to answer any questions and converse, and so I did go to his side and inquire of his Master. He did tell me of the great Christ's many accomplishments and wisdom and a voice from deep inside my heart did speak to me and I did know that it was my path to continue in His ways. So I did join with Paul's number and consent to become his student and he did teach me of the many secrets and techniques and wisdom of God. I did soon find that I was a gifted seer, though never did I share this with any, for I did see how many of the most gifted among the Disciples did meet with terrible ends. And so did I cultivate and develop my skills but kept them tightly to my breast and shared of their hearts only with those whom I could trust with my confidence.

OF MY TEACHINGS

I did begin to teach of my knowledge to the upper class women of the times, for I could gather them about me in comfortable and private surroundings away from the prying eyes and ears of the husbands and fathers who did seek to keep their hearts and minds stifled.

One occasion I do well remember was a gathering within the home of one of the noble families, and all the women were gathered there to hear me speak and teach and the man did arrive unexpectedly at home and demand to know of what was transpiring. I did smile sweetly and tell him of our secret plans to throw a party in his honor to celebrate his many accomplishments and deeds. He was a man and, of course, was won over by this simple flattery and with a jolly chuckle did command the servants to bring us anything that we might need, and so did we close the door and I did commence with my teachings of independence and freedom and the rights of women to break the yoke of the tyranny of their husbands and fathers. And so it was a wry joke on the circumstances, but one that did make us all laugh and was a good demonstration of the need I did teach of for women to begin to assume and assert their own powers.

OF THE LIONS

I was once going upon a journey to view of the regal lions that were kept for the viewing of the public that they should come to know and be educated of these ferocious beasts of power. I was with a group of my flock as we had journeyed together to partake of the experience. Something did go awry and two of the lions did escape their enclosure and set upon the crowd. My flock did flee behind me yet I did know that many would perish if I did not tame the beasts. And so as they did hungrily approach, I did use the technique for taming wild animals and did send a ball of flaming love of the Christ to envelop them completely, while I did quietly chant the sacred words and use the powers of my imagination and prayer to bring the great beasts quietly to my feet.

When I had finally subdued of their hearts and they did lie quietly beside me, I did bid them follow me back and did return them to safekeeping. Though I did eschew and disdain the public display of power or miracles, this was an exceptional occasion that did merit of its use. And so as all who had seen and known of what I had done could not keep any secrets soon had the story of my actions spread throughout the lands.

OF MY DEATH AND BETRAYAL

I did meet my fate at the hands of an angry mob of the pagan worshippers in the city of Crete where I had journeyed to aid in evangelizing there. I had gone with a few of my female companions to spread of the teachings to the circle of fine families who lived in that fair city. As we did approach, we were seized and taken by the mob of pagan worshippers. And when they did inquire of our names and purposes, one of my companions did become seized with fear and share of my identity and purpose. The pagans had already been seized with a fit of rage at the growth and prosperity of Christianity in recent years and had no qualms about taking the lives of any who did profess to know and spread of its ways and teachings.

And so my companions and I were tried and condemned of crimes against the pagan gods and were executed instantly. Our bodies were tossed in a deep ravine and found only by the wild beasts of the night, and so were we dispatched to other realms, and none were ever any wiser.

We did know that it was a dangerous thing to venture outside the protection of our circle, yet we did feel that our identities and purpose of visiting friends would protect us from any harm. I did never suspect that a deep fear and betrayal would lead me to such an ignominious end at the hands of wretched pagans. But such are the mysteries of God and HIS true ways and wisdom. And so did we have the courage to face the threat of pagan hordes, and so were we betrayed by our own number and sent to our deaths.

CHAPTER FOUR

THE RETURN
OF SPIRITUAL RELICS

❧

VORTEXES AND GROUP CONSCIOUSNESS

JESUS: A group consciousness is formed when a set or group of people do begin to share of the same thoughts, ideas, philosophy, and emotions. It is a collective memory and voice and awareness that is the sum and total of the higher true selves of all those that do exist within that state and place of awareness. It is truly similar to the collective unconscious notion proposed by learned philosophers and teachers. This group consciousness does have a voice and intelligence of its own that is directly linked to the thoughts, hearts, and energy of all who do serve it. Those who are skilled at soul travel and do know the proper methods and words may approach and converse with this consciousness voice that does represent the sum of all others. In this way might the intentions, histories, and beliefs of a group or group that does surround an object be known, for this consciousness is aware of its history and does have a memory all its own. This is the nature of a group consciousness and how it does truly function.

WORLD PEACE

CONSCIOUSNESS OF WORLD PEACE

Truly, we were created by the souls and voices of all who do share our heart and mission. We are a state of awareness and a true and just step upon the long path back to God. We do seek to end of all strife and fighting—that man should walk in peace again—though we know that this will never be. Here in this physical world, there is no place for world peace, for this would violate the balance of all divine plans. There must be negative to balance the positive, yet truly do we strive to do our duty thus. You may help our endeavors by truly teaching those who do our work how to quickly move past this phase of development, for it is a place of sanctimonious self-righteousness that souls may truly become ensnared and stuck. You can teach each to take responsibility first for his or her own example and behavior, and then shall all other desired ends quickly fall into place.

THE HOLY GRAIL

THE CHALICE AND HOLY GRAIL

JESUS: Of the Chalice and the Grail, there is this: The Chalice was that sacred Cup that the Disciples did use to drink of my blood during the Last Supper. The Grail is a stone with writing upon the edge that is the earthly incarnation that represents the consciousness of that state sometimes known as the "Universal" or "Christ" or

"Buddha consciousness." The stone was given to Peter upon his travels and later passed to Benjamin to begin the Grail Line. I did direct Peter in his dreams where it might be found, and it has remained hidden ever since. It has written upon it the names of all the knights ever to hold it in their hand, for to touch it truly does one have to be of pure heart and initiated into the Circle's ways else it shall lead to certain death. It does now reside with the Chalice in that town where both are hidden and well-guarded.

THE CONSCIOUSNESS OF THE HOLY GRAIL

The Grail was truly hidden by the last of the Grail Knights in the early fourteenth century. He was a knight named Leglens, who was of an obscure and hidden line, and few did know his true name. He hid the Grail in New England in those rocky and forbidding shores. Since that time, it has been protected by an ancient line of brothers who are dedicated to its keeping. It is near the town called Dublin. Though this would seem an unlikely place, it is truly so.

Now is the proper time for the Chalice and the Stone to be returned to their true home in Jerusalem that Christ's work and cycle might finally be completed. He has long waited for this day when all would be resolved, and He might finally go onward to His next place and mission.

The Knights who once held and protected it were of the Martel line, and Benjamin was their first. The tradition was passed down in secret through the many centuries, and this was how Europe was truly kept safe and protected. When Hitler did come and seek of the Spear for his own dark purposes, it was the Chalice and the Grail that did keep the world safe. Rudolf Steiner was one of the few who did truly see and understand. Even Winston Churchill did only have the vision to see and hear the truth when it almost was too late. Now, all must be resolved and all cycles completed that we all might go on our own way.

CONSCIOUSNESS
OF THE KNIGHTS OF THE HOLY GRAIL

Truly do we come to speak of our hearts to you. Now, we do again return to initiate new brothers into our order, for the cycle must be finally concluded, and there remains some few acts to be done. We must add one to our number to complete the final deed. The deed that must be done is to return the Holy Grail to its final resting place in Jerusalem, and this may only be done by a Knight of the Circle, for no other may truly find or touch the Cup. It must be one whom the Order will recognize and acknowledge, and truly release it to them. The Knights did follow under the leadership and patronage of the Martel Line, but as the ages did pass and our number became fewer, we did finally end our Circle on earth. Rudolf Steiner truly was the last, sent to avert the great disaster when Hitler did seize the Spear. We have since had no followers who were able to hear of our true voice or serve us in other matters.

THE SPEAR
OF LONGINUS

THE CONSCIOUSNESS
OF THE SPEAR OF LONGINUS

The Spear is a sacred relic of the Christ and was hidden after he did die but was discovered and used by all great kings of Europe to take them ever onward to greater fame and glory. Hitler did truly know this and took the Spear as his own and used it as his personal talisman of power. Though the Spear is a relic of Christ, it does have a dark side as well to balance its great power of light and the wielder may use it to either purpose. Hitler did choose the dark left path and nearly did put all the world asunder. Were it not for the Chalice and the Grail, the war would never have been won.

This is the time now that the Spear must be restored to its true home in Jerusalem, and the long cycle of Christ's time truly brought to an end. The Spear does now reside in America, for it was truly taken there after the war to keep that young nation safe from harm's great way. The relic in Austria is but a copy and has no real power. Though the Americans will not want to return it to its rightful owners, now is truly the time, and to go against the will of God in this matter will have grave and unfortunate consequences for all.

Of the Legend of the Spear, this can be said: that truly does its wielder have to bear a noble and true heart to keep it by his side and ride onward to glory for God and country. Though it may be used to evil ends, this does always finally end in disaster, and the bearer of it thus does condemn himself to countless eons of unpleasant experiences upon the wheel of reincarnation. Thus should the one who wields it take care to bear forth only with a pure and noble heart.

JESUS: Of the dark side of the Spear, there is this: The Spear was an object of power, and its essential nature was of that negative force. No light or love could rend it asunder, for that was truly not a thing that could be done—to change a thing's true purpose would be to violate the nature and balance of the Universe. Instead the Spear was imbued with great power, and it was left to the wielder which way he would choose. Hitler chose the left path, but this was not always the case. The Chalice and the Grail were of pure positive power, and this is why so much chaos has sometimes surrounded them, for if the light is not balanced by the dark within the heart of an object, then it must be balanced without.

Consciousness
of the Illuminati

The Spear is our true talisman and shall not be breached or gifted to any other, for it does guide the fate of nations and it is our true and lasting protection against the incursion and domination of others. It is here in America, and we do guard it well, but it may not be revealed or released and may not be spoken of openly. The one who brought it here did have a large and voluminous mouth, and he did pay dearly for his inability to maintain silence. We exist and do remain to keep the true Spear safe and protected, for this is our sacred duty.

The Spear has long been well-guarded and has driven this country to great glory, and it would be folly to allow it to go. We did learn of its great power from the writings of the great seer who was to be the last of the Circle Line. Steiner was truly one who could well see into the mysteries of life and beyond the veil of time. We did then add with our own studies and did learn of all the secrets that the Spear did truly bear. When the trials did begin for Hitler, we were cautious of what was said, and through our power and connections, did expunge all references to its power and true nature.

When the great American general did venture to its lair, the Spear was seen and remembered, and we did begin our plans to make it finally ours. A secret replica was commissioned and made by an ancient artist who did truly know of the secrets of those times. Then we did have the museum in Vienna closed for a secret state visit, and while its doors were locked to the public did quietly make the change while all were truly distracted on other parts of the affair.

Thus the Spear did come to be in our possession and was taken to our shores to protect us from all enemies and bind us tighter to our allies from those rocky northern shores where the other sacred relics did remain. Now the Spear is truly hidden, deep within the vaults of our marshy capitol city, and there it shall remain until the One who is truly worthy, does come to claim its heritage.

THE KNIGHTS TEMPLARS

CONSCIOUSNESS OF THE KNIGHTS TEMPLAR

Our founder and first leader, Huges de Payan, was given our name and mission in a vision by the great Archangel Gabriel who was Christ's great guide and brother from within the heavenly host. He did come to Huges and inform him of his great mission to create an Order of Knights to serve and uplift the poor and downtrodden and to truly improve their station that they might more easily move onward in their great search for God. For the angel did truly see of what treachery and power struggles would soon consume the church and did know that a true vehicle of power for the instrument of God's charitable works would be needed. And so were the Templar Knights conceived and initiated and given the blood of the Christ to serve as their totem of power.

The Knights were selected from amongst the royal families of the Martel and other lines for a clear and simple reason: These nobles were possessed of wealth and understood of its functioning and power and also were the powerful men in their own true right, and thus not further tempted by the acquisition of more of the will and nature of additional power over their fellow man. Many of the church did seek of its reins and advantage to improve their station in life and as a means of acquiring wealth and power through the hold the church did have over the many in the land of peasants and other stations. It was a good vehicle for one without nobility or rank to quickly climb in wealth, power, and stature. And so while it did truly attract and retain many good men of God, it did to its number also bring in and allow to rise many with darker motives as well.

Thus were the Knights Templar and the Grail Knights conceived and born to act as a counterbalance and true system to check the quickly growing power of the church and give some guidance and oversight to the process that the church's dictatorial powers might remain controlled and managed in the early centuries of its growth and development. For the minds and hearts of the people were more vulnerable and susceptible in those times and great protectors of the light were needed to balance the great darkness. And so were the Orders of the Knights Templars and the Knights of the Holy Grail truly conceived and born.

OF BERNARD OF CLAIVAUX'S SUPPORT AND LOVE

Bernard of Claivaux was a great and noble father who did truly serve our cause. He was one of the few within the church's number who did possess of the vision to know and see what would truly transpire in later years. And so did support our growth and formation and the recognition of our power and purpose as a healthy means to control and regulate the powers of the church, which did have the capability to grow unchecked and truly dominate every aspect of all men's lives if not kept in proper balance. Thus did Bernard sit with Huges and promise of his protection for as long as he truly could be of service, and thus were the Knights Templar born with the blessing of the church.

OF GABRIEL'S GUIDANCE OF HUGES

Huges was a soul who was known to, and did know of, the great and heavenly host who did aid the Christ in His many ways and doings. The Angel Gabriel was usually the one who did bear forth to him with messages and information on the order, function, purpose, and mission of our number. Times were different then in the nature of the planet and the ethers, and it was not so uncommon as today for one of the heavenly host to appear before a man of sight and carry on conversations or make plans or issue instructions that did support the aims of those in higher realms. And so did Gabriel come regularly in those early years to Huges and instruct him in all the ways and means of the future of our Order.

OF OUR PURPOSE AND MISSION

The Knights Templars were conceived and ordered to create a system of economic growth and development that would move the common man forward in his evolution as an independent and conscious soul. Man at this time had abdicated many of his decisions regarding his true life and sustenance and direction to the hand of his master or royal who did control the lands upon which he toiled. For his peasant class to evolve as a consciousness and develop, they did need to begin to have the mechanisms and means to control their own destinies and make their own decisions.

And so was our Order conceived and born to aid in the unfoldment of the common man by creating a system of financial balance and equality of opportunity that those below might begin to take those first tentative steps toward guiding their own destiny and taking greater responsibility for their own lives. And thus did we create what is now known as the modern banking system.

The Grail Knights did have as their mission a wholly other matter. Their purpose and duty was to keep the peoples safe from marauding invaders and intruders and to maintain justice and protection for those who had none in such troublesome and weary times where might and force did often rule in the place of higher actions. And so were the Grail Knights conceived and born of Benjamin that the lands and peoples should remain free and protected to develop as was needed and begin to return home to God.

OF JACQUES' DEATH

When King Phillip IV and Pope Clement did conspire against our Order and did truly have Jacques burnt upon the stake, they did open the doors to the great and terrible justice and fury from the heart of God himself. Jacques did lead our earthly number on a holy mission from God. And when Phillip and Clement, in full knowingness and consciousness, did turn to the darker powers and take Jacques from this plane, they did open themselves to the full and immediate fury of the wheel of retribution of cause and effect for their misdeed.

Jacques was a man of God and a talented metaphysician who did understand the workings of the laws of the inner worlds. And so as he was taking his last and final breaths, he did concentrate his powers and with the sacred words did open a channel of love deep into the heart of God and issue of his prophecy that both Phillip and Clement would end their earthly stay and not be able to enjoy or partake of the power they did seek and would join the ranks of the unborn on the inner worlds before a year had turned. This final act by one so filled with love and possessed of the power and will of God did quickly set in motion those forces of retribution for cause and effect to quickly do their work. And so did both Phillip and Clement meet with their untimely end before a year had passed. And so was Jacques vindicated in his prophecy, but we had lost a great soul and leader and in his death was sorely missed.

OF PHILLIP'S FEAR AND WEAKNESS

Phillip of France was a weak king and ruler and did fear the brightness of the light. He did know that our mission and duty was to bring greater strength and independence to those who did lie lowly about his feet. Those who were wise did see this as an opportunity to raise the level of cooperation with the masses and so work to mold and shape the system that would serve all in their highest cause. But for Phillip, this was not the way. For truly was he afraid of change and the loss of control and absolute power that he did so greatly fear. And so did he begin to show the face of rage and jealousy in many of his actions and words.

First, did he ban the nobles from joining or supporting of our number or mission. Then did he decree that all who bore our banner upon his lands would be subject to fines and imprisonment, and finally to death did he condemn any whom he did catch aiding or supporting our efforts. But this did truly work against him, for it did only stiffen the resolve of all within our number to work against an obvious servant of Lucifer. And so we redoubled our efforts to free the poor and downtrodden peoples of his lands. And so did he redouble his efforts to deter us until, in a final desperate act of darkness, he did conspire with the weakness and fear and pride of the leader Clement of the church to bring about our fall.

Of the First Banking System

The Knights of our Order did truly possess and control much of the wealth and power of Europe upon our times. We did seek of those to join our number and mission who did have the means and the wisdom and courage to truly fulfill our goals. And so at Huges' hand did we begin to acquire and accumulate wealth and devise the system of regulations and checks and measure to enable the transfer of power down to the common man. It was a system and process that did have to account for and manage the preservation of capital and the base of the operating system with fairness and efficiency, while slowly teaching and supporting and aiding those newly birthed souls in taking the next small step onward toward self-sufficiency and mastery of their own lives.

And so did we slowly toil to create distributed central repositories and vehicles of wealth and purchase and to devise the system of rules and enforcement and legal means and structure to shape the system of function and control that would be necessary to protect those who did seek to use of its resources as well as those who did possess them.

Within the inner worlds, there is an efficient system of checks and balances of cause and effect that do regulate the proper actions of soul as he does develop and grow. When an aspirant is initiated of a Master, he does for that time travel within the folds of the protection and energy of the Master's broad cloak. While he is growing and functioning under the Master's name, he is borrowing and temporarily using of the Master's power to achieve his aims or goals, and the Master has a system of instantly knowing when that power is being abused or misused, and so quickly and properly can make the necessary corrections.

So did we seek to develop a crude but functioning system that would as well enable us to regulate the functions and actions of those who did seek to utilize of the borrowed energy of financial resources to achieve their means and goals. As so, just as there are penalties of a nature of cause and effect that increase in severity with the level of the misdeed and the power that conceived it, so did we create the system and devices to manage the proper use of financial energy to truly beneficial ends. And thus were the beginnings of the modern banking system conceived.

OF THE END OF OUR MISSION

As we did grow in number and power, the church did begin to fear of our reach and capabilities, and of the wealth that we did distribute and control within the lower classes. And so did they conspire to drive us from our duties and missions and to take all that we had achieved for their own. Thus did Clement and the others seek to create a plan to overtake the system we had created for the betterment of man. But we did know of their efforts, for we were truly warned, and so did we begin to move our resources to hidden places of safety to endure the coming storm.

The system we had created was well being accepted and utilized and was growing of its own accord by those who had seen its benefit and learned to wield its ways, and so did we know that soon would our mission be slowly ending and the members of our number dispersed to other lands. So did we begin to slowly gather up our resources for our return to other duties and to leave behind what we had created for others to continue in our stead. Thus were the Catholic's plots and plans truly known and seen and thus did we prepare for what we knew was to come.

OF PRINCE HENRY'S WISDOM

Prince Henry was a great soul who did have the vision to see of the true benefit that the workings of our number would have for all of man, and so did he give us sanctuary and refuge and support to build and test the rules and regulations that would govern the modern institution of which we were planting the seeds. He did allow and assist us in implementing those reforms and educating his peoples of the power and merit and functioning of the system and how it could benefit their lives and give them greater freedom. Many were fearful and did not understand, for they were now facing a new way of thinking from one which had endured for centuries before. But with patience and time and teaching we did refine our systems and methods and begin to have success.

We did have to build our workings on the fundamental principles that the Christ had truly given as a basis for decisions and right action, for this truly was the first step. Ultimately, any system of commitment and responsibility may only successfully work if there is a shared ethic and code of honor that all do share and adhere.

Thus did we begin by first educating in a specific and orderly manner of the tenets of Christ's teachings on responsibility and truth and honor to all within his realms. Once this had been done and understood, then could we commence to freedom and the right and need of self-direction on the long road back to God and finally to financial freedom and independence as a step in this great journey home.

And thus were the peasants slowly educated, and thus were the first seeds planted and fruits harvested of our great efforts to create the system and functions that should free all men from service. And thus did the support and love and vision of Prince Henry earn for him great merit and everlasting glory in heaven for his service to God and man.

Of Our Aid to Richard

Richard was a great king who did face of many challenges to protect and keep free the many peoples of his lands, and so did he beseech of our forces and knowledge to help to make the changes and defeat the forces that did seek to avert his aims. We were called to England to aid him in his quest, and so did send a large portion of our number to go and aid him there. He was faced with the threat of tyranny from outside forces who did seek to take from him all that he had achieved by prowess and honest doings.

So when our great number did arrive, it was a sight for his heart, for he did know that truly now would the powerful forces of light and love be brought to his side to aid him in his endeavors. And so did we battle by his side and help him to defeat his enemies and return his lands and peoples to the safety of his heart and protection.

And thus was another ally won and gained and converted to the truth of our mission and cause. For after we had returned his kingdom, we did, with his consent and support, begin to teach the peoples of all that we had learned and did know of our trials and tests with Prince Henry to build the system of equality that would eventually liberate man. Also did we teach to Richard how to create and operate the great system that all should be treated fairly and that his realms might grow and prosper by the deeds and actions of those among his number as they did find their wings and soar. And so was Richard aided and converted and another ally won.

OF OUR HIDDEN WEALTH

When we did see of what was truly coming and the end of our mission and times, we did truly know that we could not leave our wealth and monies to be stolen by the church, for this would truly have created such a great imbalance of wealth and power by the forces and powers of darkness that forever would all of man's hopes and chances of growth and happiness have been stymied and put asunder. And so did we gradually withdraw and hide our riches that they should be protected until One would come to serve again the purposes of the Christ and would need of our resources to fulfill his mission and deeds.

Some were placed in secret chambers in the lands and keeps of Europe. Some were taken across the sea. And to other places is the wealth and ransom of kings truly hidden and awaiting the pure heart who should retrieve it from the depths, for it is saved and intended to serve and fuel the great next renaissance of man.

THE INSCRIPTION UPON THE STONE
OF OLD DOES READ THUSLY:

This is a sacred hiding of the power of the Templars.
It is protected and hidden from all of untrue hearts.
If one should seek its treasures, tis folly to pursue it,
for all does remain protected and hidden, save for the One true heart.

And thus was the warning placed and given to all who would seek of its treasures and were not worthy to pursue them.

IN JERUSALEM AND THE MIDDLE EAST

In Jerusalem and the Middle East did we finally spread our reaches to fulfill our missions there, for we could not end our times or days until we had completed our purpose. And so did we slowly move onward into those perilous realms to implement the systems that now we had perfected. Slowly did we approach the proper peoples and teach them of our ways to create the system of support and devices that should eventually bear all ownership and responsibility for the system once we had withdrawn and gone. And so to the Sanhedrin and other powerful orders did we teach the secrets of how to run the financial system to maintain fairness and control.

We did know that our efforts would be perverted after we were done and gone by those interested only in power and control, but this is always the case of those of lower wisdom, and the Jewish clerics were no exception. The banking system was to be an altruistic service to raise the place of man, but it is a system that does truly embody the power of the dark as well as the light, and many did choose to pervert it to its negative ends. And so did we put into place the banking and financial systems in Jerusalem and the Middle East, and so did some pervert it to evil purposes, and others to noble ends as was their each and own particular temperament and the lessons they did need to learn.

OUR FINAL ACT

Our cycle had been completed and our time had truly come when Jacques did truly perish and the end of all our number was known and we did perish from the earth. We were told by Gabriel that our mission was nearly completed and were instructed to begin our preparations and assemble our number in the Northern regions to give final aid to the king there. And so did we place our riches in hidden locations and go to Scotland to aid him in his cause, for our defense of his lands and purpose from the encroachment by foreign forces was to be our final deed. And so did we fly into battle at his side, along with many of our Grail brothers, and defeat the enemies of the King of Scots and so complete our days.

CHAPTER FIVE

THE FAMILY CIRCLE

❦

JESUS' FATHER JOSEPH

THE ESSENES

The Essenes were a secret group and I was of their number, for my brother had truly been one of them and did introduce me to their ways. It was foretold of Jesus' coming, and of mine role and Mary's, too, and I did merely use the sacred techniques to facilitate and speed the process. My teachers did know that those above did seek of a pure vessel to carry the Son of God, and so I did speak with Mary and with her agreement and consent did send the message that we would be willing to act as the host. And so was Jesus delivered cleanly into the womb of Mary, and we did begin to prepare to teach the future Son of God.

The instructions of the Essenes were very general—that Jesus was to be raised and taught as any normal boy would—except that certain characteristics of humility, independence, merit, and valor were truly to be emphasized. For it was considered important that Jesus not know or perceive that He was special lest His sense of self-importance and arrogance become inflated. And so we did raise Him quietly as any son or daughter and did teach Him an honest trade that would always allow Him to serve others, and thus did we raise our Son.

I was not as devoted to their ways and to their secret traditions as were many others, and so did I go occasionally, upon each month or so, to learn and hear the teachings. Once the Christ had been born and was truly beginning to grow and mature, it was understood that His true nature would guide Him well along the path. And so most of my time and efforts were spent giving Him the love and protection and care that any son would seek of his father, and I did not seek to give Him of the secrets of God until many years later.

The Essenes did teach at their gatherings of many similar principles to Christ, yet theirs was not a social teaching. It was more focused and concerned with the esoteric, secret knowledge of God and the universes and less with the social upliftment of man. And thus did they not care for large or voluminous numbers of followers but rather those few of great merit or deed who could truly aid their endeavors.

The Essenes were a secret order that did not meet publicly or even acknowledge each other's presence outside of their own gatherings. I did learn and know of others by when I met them there, but never was there any outward recognition or sign given to an unknown one of our number. For we did only nod or smile if there was some pressing need or purpose. The inner circle was comprised of the Master or Masters and the students, and each time we did gather, it would be to learn or practice or record of a new technique or discovery that did add to their vast knowledge of God and the universes. For it was their mission and duty to teach the other teachers and to guide and shape the society of man through the many they did advise. And so were their meetings devoted to these and other matters.

JESUS GROWING UP

Jesus was a precocious boy and given to the natural curiosities and energy and mistakes of any healthy child. He did always seek to know and understand of how all did function and why, and we did have many adventures to discover of hidden secrets in nature or about the town. I did truly give Him of love and discipline in equal measure, for it was clearly stated that He was to receive no special quarter lest His great humility and discipline be lost and His mission failed. And thus did I endeavor to raise Him as an industrious and hard working boy.

FATHERLY ADVICE TO OTHER FATHERS

I did slip quietly into the night on the eve of Jesus' leaving and before His return. When I did know He would be gone, my heart was broken, and I could no longer carry on. That my Son whom I did love and who had given so much of His heart and teachings to all of man would be so unjustly executed. And so with a heavy and broken heart did I lie upon my bed, and in my grief and sorrow did I call to the Angel Gabriel to come and take me home. And so in his mercy, and as he had long ago promised, he did come and gently lift me from the body that I might go and return to the Father's side.

THE FATHER'S PRAYER
FOR FAMILY AND HOME

Father I do come to hear,
Of YOUR true heart and teachings.

I watch over my home and family here,
And seek to do YOUR ways.

These are difficult and troubling times,
And many are the challenges.

Yet with YOUR love and trust,
We shall with strength and love succeed them.

I ask YOU now to give to me, one favor and one boon,
To keep my family safe from harm, till I shall lead them home.

MOTHER MARY

WHY JESUS WAS GIVEN TO ME

Scribe, you come to me in my hour of need to fulfill my greatest desire: that is to tell all the world of my Son's great love and of His true nature, for not of this earth was He. Those above sent Him forth from below their hidden robes that He might provide the boon for man that long had they been waiting.

He was given to me that I should bring Him forth and give the world a true Savior. Noble is His Line, unto even the depths of the beginning of time. Once, those great gods did rule the earth, and far and wide were their powers. However, they let man slip into a wayward path under their watchful eyes, and when at last the error was perceived, it had truly run its course and indeed was too late. The Son of God was given hence to atone for their grievous error. He gave His heart and love that a new dawn might be given to man and a new era of hope begun. His true love and wisdom has been bent and strewn in misuse and slander for all the ages hence. You must give forth the true essence of His teachings anew that His mission might be fulfilled.

How I Was Given Jesus

The Son of God was truly given to me cleanly. I was taken in the night beyond the confines of my body. There was I given the Seed of Light that was to birth the Savior. The Angelic Order of the Grey Robes came to me and told me of my mission: to bring forth the Son of God that He might fulfill a great mission. Whence I awoke, I knew not what had transpired but could sense a gentle presence. In several months time, I did know that the dreams had indeed been true, and I bore the Christ child within me. Silent did I have to be until He was much older. Even then in those ancient times, one could not speak of such things openly.

Jesus was a nimble boy and generous of heart and feeling. He quarreled little with any others though would not stand injustice. We taught our own until they were of age to go to public places. There they did learn of all the subjects that were the wisdom of the day. My Son neither excelled nor lingered upon the studies of the mind. Instead was His heart truly occupied with all the concerns of others. Difficult was it for He to fathom the injustices of others. His love even then was great and noble toward all.

When He finally came of age to further pursue his studies, He went abroad to search for truth and follow His great heart in search of wonders. His father was wise and knew that He must have a skill, so the Son of God chose a humble craft that would serve to shelter others. He learned the art of the carpenter that He should always be able to make His own way. Charity of others is not the mark of a man who is his own Master.

Then did He journey far and wide and seek all the great wisdom. When at last He did return, the world swarmed about Him. His great deeds were known by all about the lands, and His words did not get heard by all the hearts that needed them. He truly gave of all Himself that others might be fed and prosper. When they put Him on the Cross, there was no doubt that He had made the final gift for all whom He did love.

HOW I AND THE WORLD LOST MY SON

When I took the Son down off the Cross, His hands and feet were in tatters. The nails and stones had tore at His flesh until all was beyond fair matter. I held Him close and bandaged His hands and feet in rags to stop the bleeding. Though He was yet dead, still did the blood of His love flow onward into the heart of the earth. His life and love must have been joined to keep His works alive. Though His body was rent asunder, the love of God flowed through His hands and feet and entered the earth forever. The Spear of Cassius did enter him and create the sacred talisman. Yet this brave and noble act of compassion saved His form from destruction.

We then carried His wrapped body to the place of surrender. There did we put forth the stone to keep it safe from danger. We wept for the night, and the loss of a Mother, and for the great love now gone. Yet when we did rise again and venture forth, the body of my Son was gone. Of Mary and the Mother, I can say this: Jesus' heart was broad and saw no avarice or judgment. All were equal before His eyes and worthy of His love.

My Son Jesus Had a Son

Mary Magdalene was chastened by His great love and fell humbly to her knees. Sometimes those with the greatest pain are truly capable of the greatest loving. Jesus opened His heart to her and drew her into His chamber. There was the Second Son of God begotten and always hidden. When they did part their stealthy ways, it was then decided that for the safety of the Child, none would be told of its coming. Mary Magdalene went and hid till months had passed and the great danger was over.

The Son was raised within the arms of strangers who were well-selected. They knew not the Son of whom they bore though they were a noble family. The Martels were their name, and the Grail Line grew from them. Jesus' blood has walked the earth for ages and ages since and always have they maintained the quest for the great Chalice. Few were there who understood, or knew it then, and fewer are there now that truly do know it. The ancient kings of Europe's past have worked for the glory of His crown of thorns.

The Hiding of My Grandson

After the cave was opened anew and all had gone onward to proper places, Mary Magdalene and I did hide ourselves and repair to far away places. The Son of God was given a name, and it was Benjamin. He grew within the Martel clan and went abroad to many places. He finally did settle upon the lands that now have many faces. In France and to Europe did his line go to all the royal houses. He spread the blood of love that Europe might retain a great hope in the face of coming disgraces. The dark cloud that was to arise was seen and foretold even then.

The Grail Knights did guard the truth for many, many ages. And even when there were none left, another was sent who knew of deepest secrets. Rudolf Steiner was his name, and he had a noble lineage. He did rally the Knights of Old and help defeat the Germans. The Christ was not of Aryan blood but a mixture of all the races. He stood within as the armies fell and wept for the human races. This was His bane and greatest sorrow that ever did transpire. That so much death and wounds and sorrow should come of His lost graces.

The Spear of Cassius does indeed hold the power of destiny. Those who wear it on their side may not be defeated except by extraordinary measures. Steiner truly did more than is known in defeating the great black monster. His heart was pure, and bright was his light, and guided by many Masters. And the clarity and truth of his teachings and thought and new ideas were given to him by those of Jesus' inner Circle above who do truly guide all in matters of importance such as these.

Mary Magdalene and I did depart and sought shelter in Western lands. To Judea did we flee to seek shelter amongst the heathens. There did none revere the Christ or need to feel ill toward Him. We were forgotten until the day when we could resume our places hidden deep within the hills, we lived as simple farmers. We did work upon the soil and shared in menial labors. Great was our love for the rich earth that now held the love of my Son's ethers. His grace was gone, but still remained His gentle touch and essence.

After the time of several years, we came again back to the living. Unto the city did we go to seek news of all the matters. Then did I find that Benjamin was well and with a worthy family. The Martels did love him well and treated him as their own. Mary Magdalene knew that all was well, and the Second Son was well taken. We did resume our simple lives and remembered always the teachings. When our time did come, we looked within and saw Him there to guide us. My only Son had called us forth and gently stayed beside us.

My Adoptive Family

John and Mary Magdalene were two great souls who did give their hearts unto my service to honor of the Christ and their pledge to Him to always be of His great service. John was a gentle and loving soul and did dote on me and protect and serve me as if I were his own. He never did leave me unattended by himself, or Mary Magdalene, or some other whom he did trust for fear that I might need something or experience some discomfort, and this he had sworn to the Christ I never should befall. And thus did we spend many years together at each other's sides, traveling the lands and spreading the Word of my Son to all who did care to come and hear. This, too, is the reason that John was so careful and did have such a long life, for it was his solemn duty to protect the women of his Savior after He had done and gone. And so John, Mary Magdalene, and I did spend many enjoyable years together.

Mary Magdalene was a true saint and angel and was devoted to Christ's ways and to my happiness and peace of mind. Never did she leave my side for one single day after my Son had died and gone, and she did consider it her sworn duty and mission to make sure that I did lack for no comfort to show her devotion and commitment to the Christ and to their son.

Benjamin did often come to see us, though his family knew not the true reason, but did only think that as a devoted Christian, he was truly dedicated and enamored of the Mother of Christ, and thus did we all pass many days of happiness and joy together. And we did help to train him and plan for the growth and development of the noble Grail Line and tradition, for he was a boy and did need of a mother's firm hand who did know and understand of what he was experiencing. And thus were we by his side during his trials and training for knighthood and thus did Mary Magdalene instruct him in the wiles and ways of a woman's heart that he might find success in the noble courts of Europe to plant the seeds of his line.

Mary Magdalene was truly a wonderful mother to behold and always did it greatly pain her not to be able to claim her true son. But she did understand and see the bigger picture, and so did honor her promise to the Christ to keep the secret with her, and so did take it truly to her grave. Mary Magdalene did repent well of her earlier ignorance and misunderstandings and did command herself as a true saint and lover of a Savior for the rest of her earthly days. Though Jesus was a Savior and a King, He was also still a man and not immune to the charms of a beautiful and talented woman of which Mary Magdalene did have many. And so as the days and years did pass, she did prove herself worthy of His confidence and more as her deportment, actions, and demeanor did guide her truly as a saint. Thus was it like to live and love and travel with John and Mary and my grandson Benjamin.

THE ROLE OF WOMEN IN MY TIME

Women in this time and age were not permitted religious freedoms and were given no voice in the affairs that governed the institutions of worship and higher teachings. I, although I was the Mother of the Savior, was still given little voice or formal recognition of authority within His group of followers though I did have a significant and sophisticated level of development and achievement in the ways of the spiritual life. But it was widely held and considered by those weak men who did fear of losing their power that the influence of women beyond the family walls would poorly bode for the well being of society, and thus were we allowed no say or voice. 'Twas a great misjudgment of worth and valor on their part, which did later cost them many lives as the errors of the Sanhedrin did return to haunt those peoples in many later times.

TO THE WOMEN OF TODAY

The women of today truly do not know or understand the broad scope of freedom that they truly do enjoy. To be able to travel freely, to own their own possessions, to speak their mind and bear authority without any fear of repercussion truly are incredible and marvelous, and long overdue things. In matters of state, the freedoms and accomplishments of women truly have done well.

In matters of the church, however, this is another matter. The Catholic church today does owe much of its suffering and mistreatment of its innocent flock to the imbalance and undue influence of male power that has accumulated over the past centuries and days. Man of himself—that is the male of the species—cannot create a balanced organization and channel for God if the female aspect is not acknowledged, respected, and integrated. For without its balancing influence, all does eventually become perverted to the extreme, which is what has happened today.

A stronger female influence within the leadership of the formal church hierarchy is truly necessary to restore the faith of the flock and rejuvenate and rebuild the truth and teachings of the Christ else all will continue to slowly cycle down and decay until truly is nothing left. The church does have a great and important opportunity to right the wrongs of years of injustice, and this is the first true step. There are many women of accomplishment and merit within those hallowed halls whose voices and opinions do need to be heard and considered, and the Vatican must begin to allow their number to start to call it home. Thus might greater misfortune and calamity be avoided and the long road of healing begun.

MARY MAGDALENE

I will tell you much of the true heart of the matter and of His early travels. Far and wide did He go to find the Word of God. From the scattered teachings of truth did He, bit-by-bit, construct the great work that now bears His name. No one truth is all complete, and the Son of God well knew this. Each of its own possesses those few parts that were right for its time. Others who followed have perverted the true word to their own ends by adding their own phrases. Thus was it with the word of Christ. He did truly find what He sought hidden amongst the pillars of time and pyramids of the desert. Even to the Himalayas did He go to learn from the adepts there. The Christ knew that none could possess all the truth and so searched far and wide until He had His teachings.

A HARD LIFE

When I was a young girl, I was abandoned by my family who did flee Jerusalem to seek of better opportunities outside the city gates. I did have five brothers and sisters, and as I was the eldest, I was left to fend for myself and survive of my own devices. Jerusalem was not a pretty or safe city then, and I was a girl gifted with a fair face and beauty, and the attraction and attention of men was truly a thing that came naturally.

I did seek at first of employment in a shop or place of eating and drink, but none would give shelter or sustenance to a girl without a family, and so did I find myself alone upon the streets. Many were there who did offer to take me in and make me their wife or private lover, yet none did meet my fancy or turn the doors of my heart.

And so I did decide to use what was in my favor on the terms and conditions that were mine. And thus did I become a lady of the night but remained my own person and steward of my own fate. For to me to share of my body in a quick and mindless way for profit was a much better alternative and truer course of action than to be taken roughly in the street or bar at any soldier's whimsy and so left to face the shame and self-loathing that did accompany such an act. And so I made my decision to be the master of my life and did work and do as I pleased and answered to none but myself.

JESUS, THE MAN

Jesus was a different man from any I did know for more reasons that I can count or remember. I did see Him first as He was speaking in the street to a group and there was something in His countenance and posture and stature that I could not tear my eyes from His face. My heart did burst forth with a depth and breadth of love the likes of which I had never known, and I did truly know that this would be the first, last, and only man whom I would ever love.

I did follow Him after He was done speaking but did not approach to speak, for I was afraid that one as beautiful and loving and kind and handsome as He would find no favor with a lady of the night. But He did sense my presence and turned to speak to me and I did suddenly find myself in His hands and looking to His face. His blue eyes were of the deepest oceans and sparkled with a loving intensity that did weaken me at the knees. His strong jaw and nose and cheeks were the features of a noble though He did wear of common dress. He was of average height and build, and had brown and wavy hair, but when He did smile and show His mouth, I did begin to sway and He did have to hold me that the stars before my eyes might have led me to the ground. He did ask of my name, and kindly gave me His, and then with a gentle smirk and smile and a twinkle of His eye did He bid me farewell and hoped we would meet again.

I did rest upon the street for many long and forgotten minutes, and then did return to my place to think and reflect on this remarkable man. For I had know of many men, the most powerful in all the lands, yet none did have the power and presence of love that was borne within Jesus' breast. I did return on the morrow and for many days after to hear Him speak and teach, and gradually did I come to understand and know and become skilled in the ways and techniques that He did share.

He would always answer all my questions patiently and with His loving smile and bid me return again to continue our conversations. And never did He hint or mention or suggest of any desire other than to teach me of the ways of God. Finally, after many months of speaking I did suggest that I should like to prepare for Him a meal to thank Him for His many kindnesses, and thus did we meet and share a tender evening and I was able to return of the love that He had so tenderly given to me so freely.

Jesus was a private man with His innermost emotions and feelings and though He did love and give of all His heart to all who did truly need it, it did take a mighty toll upon His body and emotions, for none were there but I with whom He could share of the things that truly bothered and frightened Him. And so did we develop a close and loving friendship. And He did never judge me or any other for my ways or my decisions, and I did become converted and devoted to His teachings and His service and thus did we share many happy times.

OF MEN AND WOMEN

There is within man a basic divisiveness between his male and female components. Soul is truly both as one, yet when the soul does enter into the body and assume one sex or another, it does forget of its other half though it does long to return to it. And so it is an unfortunate characteristic of the male energy to seek dominion over all it does encounter, and this does truly include control over all women. It is as much a basic factor of the male energy as it is of society or culture, for the standing and place of women to change there must be an evolution and growth of the male energy to accept and respect its female aspect as one equal and valid to its own.

This is a difficult thing to do, for the male mind does fear this as weakness, yet it does not realize that this does require greater valor and merit than simply ruling by brute force over the weaker sex. This was the secret the Christ truly knew and embodied that did make Him so desirable to all the women. As man does evolve and grow, this will gradually happen as a part of the natural progression and unfoldment of soul, but until that time does truly come, we must rely on our own measures.

Women today, and of my times as well, did truly find ourselves in our position because we were willing to accept it. Women have always underestimated their strength because of their natural avoidance of conflict and inability to organize and coalesce their power. Man cannot live without the comfort and care of women. But women must have the strength of character and will to know what they do desire and go and seek it thus as a single force and purpose. Thus will favor and progress be won to aid us on our course.

THE PLIGHT OF WOMEN

For women to progress in church authority it is a similar matter. Men have long stood on the authority of the Christ as a man to justify their position. But I did know of all the Disciples and Jesus did tell me as well that I was as disciplined and as learned and as accomplished as any of their number. But I did not desire to follow of their path, and Jesus did truly know that the fabric of Jewish society of that day would have buckled and torn at the thought of my coming as a herald and teacher, and so did I remain in the shadows. But this is all to say that the men of the church have no merit or authority to deny the women of their proper station and achievement, but for the fact that the women are taught to be docile and are willing to accept it.

God comes to those of bravery and valor, not to the timid or meek of heart. HIS is a favor and glory won of action, not received of hiding and pining. And so I do say this: that the women of the church can seize and rise to the power and position they do desire at any given moment. They must only decide that it is to be so, and then do it.

THE ROLE AND STATION OF WOMEN

The role and position of women in ancient times did require of many sacrifices to survive. Men did control the means of safety, sustenance, and shelter. And women did not possess of the means or courage to organize and so rise above their station, and so they did suffer quietly and make of many sacrifices. Women did do all the work about the house and for the children in addition to preparing and caring for the men in any way required. A woman was bound by law to do of her husband's wishes. Such were the tyranny of the sex in those difficult times. A man simply did own his wife and could treat her as he pleased, and in a society of martial law and foreign soldiers, the men of Jerusalem did vent their anger and frustration upon their loving wives. So women did sacrifice of all desires merely to survive and rarely did receive of education or other cultural training except of the noble houses. And thus were the many difficulties faced by women of those times.

My Evangelism

Although I was given no formal recognition for my achievement or my merit, I did truly teach to downtrodden women who did seek of my counsel and wisdom. Many were there who did have a strong desire and intuitive understanding of the nature of the Christ's teachings, and I did share with them of what I did learn and know and receive of at Jesus' knee. Often did I speak of love and courage and valor and of the many gifts that awaited them in heaven, for these were a lot that needed most of hope and a kind word to live on. And so to know that there was at least one man who did believe and teach of love was sufficient for many to carry them through their day. And so did I teach and speak and do what I could to lift the poor and lowly women of those times.

A Single Mother

When I did meet Jesus and truly learn of His mission and purpose, I did early on know that my one true love would be fleeting and fiery and eternal, and never would I love again in this life. And so when He was put upon the Cross, I was prepared and had already accepted that this would one day happen. He did come to my side before it had transpired and spoken to me and given me of His everlasting promise of devotion and to always watch over me and our son and to keep us from harm's way. And so did I go and comfort the Mother Mary and with her spend the rest of my days.

Of Benjamin, it was much harder, for he remained in flesh and blood and as he grew older did come to visit often. But it was the sacrifice I made and price I paid for loving the Son of God. Many were the nights when I was tempted to go and return him to my side, but I did always remember Jesus' words of the great and important role that our son was to play in the history and safety of man, and I could not come to put my own selfish desires above those of the world. And so with a heavy heart did I seek solace in my efforts and devotion to Jesus' teachings and Mother Mary's side.

On Single Motherhood

To raise a child without a father is a daunting task that requires the bravest of hearts and resourcefulness. The modern teachings of the Church do not well give of sufficient truth to guide a young one along the path to certain greatness. However, to the single mothers of today, I do say this: to take the words of Christ and the Disciples, and the Divine Laws contained within these pages, and add to it the truths that your heart does find within the covers of the Bible, then this will truly give you the skills to well raise a son or daughter who does understand of love and Divine Law and of the importance of each. And these truly are the most important considerations to raising a good and loving child.

Of What I Learned from Jesus

Before I met Jesus, I did live a life devoted solely to my own happiness at whatever cost to any other, and I truly did not understand the repercussions or implications of cause and effect of my actions, or why I did find myself in positions as often as I did. Jesus' teachings opened in my eyes and heart the keys to other means and ways of action that did create love and benefit for all and did make for a more harmonious and pleasant life. And so did I use of His techniques and teachings in every area of life and it did benefit me well.

A FAVORITE PRAYER

JESUS: Mary Magdalene was a beautiful soul that did never receive of the fame and glory she did rightly deserve for her contributions. This prayer was her constant reminder to herself of the great love that she bore me and our son Benjamin, and it is given to the world that all might know of the truth of her heart and her dedication and sacrifice that she did make for the love and service of God.

MARY MAGDALENE: My favorite prayer to the Christ, which I did repeat daily, was this:

> *Dear Friend and Lover, I do always miss Your heart,*
> *For I do stumble and toil, without Your guiding hand.*
>
> *My heart is broken and crumbled,*
> *As You have gone and left.*
>
> *Yet I toil in Your labor,*
> *To honor our son and love.*
>
> *I do my best at strength and courage,*
> *Yet often am I weakest,*
>
> *And seek to find Your arms again,*
> *When across the veil I seek you.*

This was the tender prayer that I did repeat daily for my lost friend and lover.

THE RETURN TO MY BELOVED

When I did finally pass away, I was an old and tired woman. I had lived for many years, and seen of many things, and gladly did I shed this shell and go on to the other side. I did remain in Mary's home by the sea in Galilee and did teach of all who sought me there of the many things I had seen. When at last I truly knew my final days had come, I called one last time to my true love and quickly He did come. I gently lay upon the bed, and folded hands upon my breast, then did I softly call His name, and feel His gentle presence. And as I did draw my final breath, He did appear before me, and swept me up into His arms that we never should again be separated. And thus was I finally returned home to the strong and gentle arms of my beloved in Heaven.

BENJAMIN MARTEL

I am truly the first of the noble line that came from the great Master. With the Martels was I hid and they did truly raise me as one of their own. I lived well and had many joyous adventures, and our family spread far and wide to create a legacy of love and truth throughout Europe's palaces. All were not perfect, and some did go astray, but the blood of our Father does run purely through us.

Of my mother, I can say this: that proud was I to be of one with such great grace and courage. I did find out who I was of, and many nights did I miss her. My Father truly saw no prejudice in His eyes and held all equal before Him and worthy of His love. He was a man I greatly did respect and always did think well of.

The Martels were a noble line and of pure and gracious hearts. They took me in and kept me safe and greatly were rewarded. My travels were broad, and many were the places I did visit. I bore no hatred for the Romans, for that would have dishonored His true teachings. The man who died only for love could not be remembered with any hatred in my heart. I did know that I was his Son, and indeed what my true mission was: to create a line of Grail Knights to protect all those whom He had not been able to reach. His work and love had to live on through my blood, and I was honored and humbled to thus serve Him. When it came time for me to pass, inwardly did I seek Him, and like a true Father He did come, and bore me away gently in His arms.

THE INCEPTION
OF THE GRAIL KNIGHTS

The Grail Knights were given to me by the coming of the Angel Gabriel who did come to me in quiet contemplation and explain of my history and destiny. I did not initially believe of his words of who was my true Father, but he did give me proof that I never could deny. He did name the Mother Mary Magdalene as the one who had truly born me, and that she was the only love of Christ, and so I did seek her and Mother Mary where they did live and hide. And thus did I ask of them directly if I were truly of their Line, and they did not lie but told me affirmatively that I was truly of the Christ.

I did return with my head quite shaken to my adopted family's home and for some time said not anything and debated how to proceed. Thus was it that the Angel Gabriel did appear to me in quiet contemplation and explain to me of my mission. I was not to tell my family yet, for the danger was yet too great but was to proceed amongst the royal families of Europe and strengthen ties with each and create true and friendly relations with all the fair ladies of those lands that the Martel line might grow long and lengthy, and thus the protection of Europe be provided against the dark forces which would arise. My line of heirs and descendants were to form that noble circle of defenders known as the Grail Knights, and I was truly their first. This did mean truly that we were to be trained in the virtuous arts and secrets of God to use the subtle powers and techniques to truly protect of all man against evil and unnatural ways.

And thus did the angel teach me of the many secret techniques, and I did learn them well that I should truly pass them along to my sons and others of the Order that the knowledge and wisdom and power never should be lost. And thus was the Grail Stone created and given in a dream to Peter to truly be delivered to me that its power as an earthly totem might forever bind and connect our line to this earth. It has an awesome power that does truly repel all darkness from those who do protect it and also hold it near.

HEAVENLY ASSISTANCE

As I did begin my training, the angel would come to me each night in quiet reflection and would instruct me via his thoughts and direct transmission of the great knowledge all that I would truly need to know to be the first of the vanguard of great protectors that would keep the darkness at bay for the next 2,000 years until the great Christ's cycle and mission truly would be complete. And so it was commenced thus and the pathway to supreme enlightenment and power within the mystic and secret ways was given to me truly that I might initiate and teach all who would follow me how to grasp and wield the power to keep all lands safe. Thus was it important for me to father many sons within the royal families and beyond, for these would form the ranks and seeds from which the great protectors would be born, and thus did I father eight sons who did go onward to other royal houses, and thus did the Martel line and others begin the legacy of greatness and glory that does surround them to this day.

The trials of the Grail Knights were rigorous and were truly designed to guide the aspirant gradually and truly through the many levels and stages of unfoldment until at last their name did come to be seen upon the Stone of the Grail and the top of the mountain was reached. Then would the Knight have the power, wisdom, and discipline to truly wield the great force of God for the betterment and protection of man.

MY SPIRITUAL ADVENTURES

I did upon my many journeys and adventures begin to create a series of monasteries that did exist by the benevolence and generosity of the Martels and others, and there were these holy Knights trained to carry out their duties. Once thusly trained and knighted, they did carry out the work of the light in both the inner and outer worlds, for there is no difference between the two, and all that does transpire below truly does have its seed and origin above. And so the great Knights did fight off invaders and evil tyrants with all their skills and weapons, and thus was Europe protected for 1,000 years and more.

At last, however, the knowledge and power of the royal circle did slowly begin to fade as the cycle of our time and mission began to draw to a close until our current age. Rudolf Steiner truly was the last of our Line sent forth to fight the great evil wielded by the One who bore the Spear. And thus was Hitler finally defeated by the last of our great Line and by those powers who did truly wield the power of the Chalice and the Grail. The time of our duty and service now has come to a close, and the relics must be returned to whence they started to end the current age.

The Chalice and the Grail Stone must be returned to Israel that they might find their true and final resting place and home else their power and light and protection should start to reverse its polarity and bring great ruin and fall to those who do refuse to relinquish them. They were mighty totems when it was truly their time, but now that time does pass and to linger does bring only folly. This is the story of the Grail Knights, whom I did love one and all.

JOSEPH
OF ARIMATHEA
(30 A.D.)

I was a friend and teacher of Benjamin in the ways of secret lore and teachings of the hidden mystical orders. I had also been a friend and teacher of his Father though this is not known or shared, for I was in the service of the heavenly hierarchies as well but with a different mission and purpose. I did know from the Angel Gabriel what was the mission and fate to befall the Grail Line of Protectors and also of the great invasion of darkness that would befall the world at the hands of the Wielder of the Spear near the years of the twentieth century. And so had the broad brush strokes of the destiny of kings and nations been writ upon the stars, and so did I know that the great Chalice and the Stone must truly reside in England to secure its protection there.

After Benjamin had been initiated and held the Grail Stone at his heart, we did venture off to England to seek of those who would protect it there. There was a secret Order of the mystical Brotherhood of old there that had truly agreed to aid in the service of the Christ's great mission in support of the plans and destinies that truly had to be fulfilled to maintain proper balance in the universe that the unfoldment and development of man might proceed as had been established. And thus their Order at Glastonbury did solemnly swear an oath to always protect the relics and keep them in their care.

This Order was called the "Monks of Sacerbury." This was a line of a different order that had been hidden and working for 1,000 years before the Christ did arrive but whose works and oral traditions were kept closely guarded and veiled from fearful public eyes but who truly had guided the earliest years of human history and development within those lands around Europe and the eastern provinces of Asia and India and China. Thus did I deliver to them of the Grail Stone for their safekeeping and protection. They were truly selected for their deep and wise ways and knowledge of the truth of men's hearts, for they were to be the Keepers of the Stone and would only allow those of pure heart to truly touch its edges and receive of the Final Gift. Thus did the Stone gradually fade into hidden history and legend, and Camelot did pass and the many other Knights did slowly move onward to other ways. The last to touch its edges and read of what is written there was the great seer and mystic Rudolf Steiner who came to save Europe and the world from the dark forces of the Spear. And thus did the Grail Stone come to be in England and protected by those who serve there.

The Blood of Christ

When the Christ was raised upon the Cross and His side was truly pierced, He did bleed the blood of heaven that fell upon the earth. This was an important occurrence, for it did imbue within the physical body of the earth the great love of His presence that it would truly endure and flourish for the next 2,000 years. But there also was another purpose, and I did gather of His blood and collect it in the sacred vessel that has been hidden lo these many years.

It was also known that the Grail Knights would have an Order of Brothers to carry out the duties of the greater plans of destiny, and so was the blood of Christ collected and later placed in the care of the Templar Order to aid them in their duties. The Knights Templar did have as their responsibilities the protection of the weak and poor, and their expertise in wealth and money was designed to serve those ends. Thus was the blood of Christ given to aid them in their tasks, for His blood was the medium of His Line and power and ability to do of great deeds when used in the proper manner.

But like any vessel of the lower worlds, it did possess within itself the great opposite negative power as well if that was truly decided to be expressed. And so did the blood of Christ represent the circulation and flow of His power within the earthly realm. And thus was the financial expertise and power given to the Templars that they would use the power of the light within its substance to create on earth the conditions and circumstances favorable to the betterment of life for all man and thus aid him in his quest for the glory of God, for it is truly a difficult challenge to seek of the love and glory of God when you haven't even any food or shelter or water.

And thus did I collect the blood of Christ and seal it tightly in its container as Gabriel did instruct me and create the talisman of power that would guide the Templar Order. He did say to me that it would be 1,000 years before those who would seek to wield it would walk upon the earth. And so he did guide me to hide it in a treasure house of the king where he did know it would be found, but not known, and later buried as the invaders came to seize of Jerusalem.

And so the Cup was buried with much other great treasure before Israel did fall. And later Gabriel did guide Huges to return and start the Order of the Templars in the Temple there and unearth of the great riches that lay hidden secretly below that did contain, among them, the mighty golden goblet that did hold the blood of Christ.

THE GIFT OF THE SHIELD TO KING MONDRAIN OF SARRAS

The Shield was a gift of light to protect his set upon peoples. Long had they suffered the effect of prior misdeeds, and it was truly time to right the imbalance of darkness. And so did we travel to his lands to bestow the gift of light. The Shield was imbued with the power to protect its wielder, and thus as it was handed down through the generations and through the families did it bring great fame and glory to all who did carry it righteously into battle.

OF MY PASSING

I did slip quietly into the night in the year that you do mention, but it was not to Glastonbury that I did retire. I did die upon the lands of France in a small town to the south were I did reside quietly to pass my final years. I had done of my great service, and did wish to end my time in quiet contemplation and repose, and thus did finally slip quietly into the night with my family by my side, and they did secretly commit me to the ground in an unmarked grave as had been my desire and wishes, for I did see how the bodies of saintly men were treated and did wish no part in that process or ritual. And so did I finally pass in that small town where miracles and tears do now sometimes occur, and some have called it "Lourdes" in these our modern times. And thus did I end my earthly service and return to the Father's side.

MY SON

My son did continue with our works and duties though his role and heart were of a lesser order. And he did wish to remain obscured and hidden and led the simple life he did favor. And thus did he spend his days doing small deeds and errands for those whom we did serve but never with the fervor or dedication that I did possess in my heart for doing the work of God.

MY FINAL WORDS

JESUS: This book is my gift of love to all who do follow of my ways and teachings. I do see of the difficulties and challenges and trials of pain and suffering that you each do face daily, and I give you these my words and those of the Disciples and my family to ease your hearts and give hope to end the suffering. Study well of the wisdom that has been here recorded, and take it into your heart, and you shall see great miracles and wonders about you as the love of God does enter into your heart and remove of all impurities and imperfections. You are each sons and daughters of God and HE does long to see you return to HIS loving arms. This book of the Scribe does have many keys and great truths to aid you on your journey. I have given of my heart and love as my gift and final offering. I send to you the love and hope of my heart to guide you on your journey home to heaven.

My love and blessings to you always.

Amen.

We hope this Jodere Group book has benefited you in your quest for personal, intellectual, and spiritual growth.

Jodere Group is passionate about bringing new and exciting books, such as *Voices from Ancient Bethlehem*, to readers worldwide. Our company was created as a unique publishing and multimedia avenue for individuals whose mission it is to impact the lives of others positively. We recognize the strength of an original thought, a kind word, and a selfless act—and the power of the individuals who possess them. We are committed to providing the support, passion, and creativity necessary for these individuals to achieve their goals and dreams.

Jodere Group is comprised of a dedicated and creative group of people who strive to provide the highest quality of books, audio programs, online services, and live events to people who pursue life-long learning. It is our personal and professional commitment to embrace our authors, speakers, and readers with helpfulness, respect, and enthusiasm.

For more information about our products, authors, or live events, please call (800) 569-1002 or visit us on the Web at **www.jodere.com**.

JODERE
GROUP